ANCIENT SECRETS

VILLARD ⬥ NEW YORK

ANCIENT SECRETS

Using the Stories of the Bible to
Improve Our Everyday Lives

RABBI LEVI MEIER

ISBN 0-679-44951-5

Random House website address: http: //randomhouse.com/

Printed in the United States of America on acid-free paper

2   4   6   8   9   7   5   3

First Edition

Book design by Jo Anne Metsch

With love and blessings
to our children,

Chana, Yosef Asher, Malka Mindel, and Yitzchak Shlomo

"Turn it over and over again—
for everything is contained within it."

—*Ethics of the Fathers*

Acknowledgments

FROM MY CHILDHOOD ON, SOME SPECIAL PEOPLE HAVE HELPED GUIDE me along my journey, and I would like to express my gratitude to them.

The greatest influences on me during my formative years were my parents, Alfred Meier of blessed memory, and Frieda Meier; my grandfather who lived with us, Julius Meier; and my teachers. I would like to single out three of my early teachers: my dear brother, Rabbi Menahem Meier; my study partner, Rabbi Solomon Polachek; and Rabbi Joseph B. Soloveitchik, of blessed memory.

During my young adult years, my Jungian analyst, Dr. James Kirsch, was a powerful influence in my life and assisted me in the development of my unconscious. Much of what is written in this book comes from that place, from that source.

During my professional life, I have learned from my students, private clients, and hospital patients, who have shared with me the most intimate details and struggles of their lives. They have all become my teachers. I would like, however, to single out one patient, Dr. Erwin Altman. I was privileged to be his rabbi for the last few years of his life. During that time, he and his younger brother, Dr. Manfred Altman of London, England, who took care of him during those years, became my inspiring guides and friends. Manfred continues to be of significant importance to me.

I would like to acknowledge the tremendous assistance of Paula Van Gelder, who has assisted me in all my writings since my arrival on the West Coast in the early 1970s. Her expertise in writing is matched only by her kindness.

I want to express my deep gratitude to Uriela Obst, who played a pivotal role in the development of this work. Her creative artistry was invaluable in helping me weave together factual material and anecdotes in a cohesive, engaging manner.

I would also like to thank friends and colleagues who have read and improved upon the manuscript, including Kenneth M. Chasen, Julie R. Korenberg, M.D., Ph.D., Lillian Lasker, Kenneth Leeds, M.D., Sharon Mars, Maureen Mercury, Janet Offel, and Fred Rosner, M.D.

I want to express my gratitude to my literary agent, Alan Nevins at Renaissance, who has become a treasured friend and colleague.

I want to thank David Rosenthal, president and publisher of Villard Books, and Annik La Farge, vice president and associate publisher at Villard, for their pioneering vision and personal encouragement. I would also like to extend my deep thanks to the dedicated staff at Villard: Lynn Anderson, Benjamin Dreyer, Ruth Fecych, Deborah Foley, Brian McLendon, Melissa Milsten, Adam Rothberg, E. Beth Thomas, and Jennifer Webb.

Together with my wife, Marcie Joy, I have dedicated this book to our children. This dedication is symbolic of our love and blessings for them.

Contents

Introduction

ONCE UPON A TIME AND FAR, FAR AWAY . . .

About 3,200 years ago—which is to say, ages before the glory of Greece or the grandeur of Rome, about a millennium before the rise of Christianity and nearly two millennia before Islam, and so long ago that neither the Babylonian nor the Persian empire had yet made its mark—a young man who held a high position in the court of the Egyptian pharaoh abandoned his wealth and his position in response to a call from a divine voice.

This unusual man climbed a mountain in the desert. We will never know exactly what happened to him there, but when he came back down, he told the people who were with him that God had spoken to him and given him the answer to every question about life that he had, that they had, and that their descendants would ever have. And the people were awed.

Then he recorded the basics of what he had been told on the mountain, writing on animal skins that were rolled up into scrolls.

When he was finished, he called his people around him and began to explain to them what he had written. He told them that if they listened carefully and did what he taught them, they would understand the meaning of life.

Does this sound like the opening of a novel, a sequel perhaps to a recent fiction best-seller about ancient parchments found in the mountains of Peru?

It isn't.

This story is true.

I am talking about Moses and the origins of the Bible—the Five Books of Moses.

Herein lies the foundation of three of the world's great religions.

Herein lie the stories of creation, of Adam and Eve, of Cain and Abel, of humanity's first struggles on earth, of the destruction by flood and the salvation of Noah, of Abraham's first pact with the one God and the dream of Jacob's ladder. Herein lies the monumental story of the slavery in Egypt, the escape, the covenant at Mount Sinai, the Ten Commandments—the codification of the laws by which humankind was to live—the wanderings through the desert, and Moses's farewell to his people as they set off for the Promised Land.

For Jews, the Five Books of Moses are the Torah—the teachings conceptually similar to the U.S. Constitution—with which all new thought and new prescriptions must agree or they are not "constitutional."

Christians regard the Books of Moses as part of their Bible. Muslims also revere many precepts found in these teachings. So it is a most important book to a very large segment of humanity.

But how many of us have really read the Five Books of Moses? And if we *have* read them, how many of us can say we really *understand* them?

No wonder: Moses was writing in a kind of shorthand, recording what was most important. He explained the rest orally, and we are taught that the obligation rested on the prophets and sages who followed him to continue to explain how the original teachings applied to new situations in the world. Thus the original writings have now generated thousands of volumes of explanations.

But how can one wade through all that has been written and find what he or she needs to know in order to answer the questions of daily life? Can it be done? Where does one begin?

I suggest we approach the original text with an open heart and mind, allowing it to work its inspirational magic, and see what happens. I have written this book to illustrate how we can draw on these ancient writings and find in them the answers to the problems of our daily lives. Today. In the modern world. The examples you will find here come from my own experiences as a Jungian psychologist, teacher, hospital chaplain, and rabbi, and from the lives of my clients, my patients, and members of my Bible study groups. I hope that through these examples you will see how it is possible to make use today of something that was written more than 3,000 years ago. But most of all, I hope that you will begin to see this ageless source as approachable and that you will begin to make *your own* very personal connection with it. This is essential.

Nowhere in this book do I mean to imply that I, or the people whose stories I tell here, have found all the answers. Your answers will be your own; they must be.

Too many of us make the mistake of relying on someone else's simplification or generalization, as if one size could fit all. It never does. There are no shortcuts. Those who think they've found them end up frustrated and depressed, stuck in blind alleys.

This book is for people who are tired of blind alleys, who are drawn to finding a truer path, who innately feel that the answers lie at the source but don't know how to unlock its ancient mysteries. They feel the Bible's magnetic pull because instinctively they sense its power. But it seems such an overwhelming task to really delve into it. It's not called the Big Book for nothing.

Yet the core of the Bible, the Five Books of Moses, is really quite small, containing only about 350 pages.

Unfortunately, the English translations generally available contain numerous inaccuracies. These texts have traveled from Hebrew to Greek to Latin before finally making it into English. In some respects, the errors can be excused; after all, some words and phrases are simply not translatable. For example, the Bible in the original Hebrew refers to the various aspects of God using words that appear to be masculine (*Adonai*), feminine (*Shekhinah*), or plural (*Elohim*). We have all capitulated in accepting the masculine form due to the limitations of the English language, as I have also done in this book, but this is not uniformly so in Hebrew.

Therefore, I would encourage anyone who has the inclination to learn biblical Hebrew; a number of good self-study guides exist. But since I suspect most of you will not, I recommend that you purchase one of the translations made directly from the Hebrew that are listed in the bibliography at the back of this book.

One word of caution: An ancient adage suggests that there are seventy ways of reading the Bible, one for each year of one's life. Why? Because it will never seem the same—as you learn and grow, this most revered of books will reveal shades of meaning and convey new understandings for which you were not ready before. The questions you ask tomorrow will differ vastly from those you ask today. But every reading will be worth it, because therein lie all the answers.

PART I

1

As in the Beginning, So Now

So LET'S START AT THE BEGINNING. HOW DOES THE MOST ancient of ancient stories—the first of the Five Books of Moses, the Book of Genesis—begin?

"In the beginning, when God began to create heaven and earth, the earth was unformed and void, with darkness over the surface of the deep and a wind from God sweeping over the water."

The image is one of desolation and despair. It makes you shiver. It feels cold, dark, and lonely. It brings to mind those moments of despair when you have felt lost, could not see any order in the chaos of your life, and felt as if you couldn't go on. Perhaps in those darkest of moments, the most appealing answer was death. And that is clearly the image that is meant to be conveyed here.

But how does the story continue? *"God said, 'Let there be light,' and there was light."*

Light—the answer to darkness. Yet could God really be creating light the way we understand it—as a source of illumination? That doesn't make much sense, since it's not until thirteen sentences later, on the fourth day, that we are told that God created the sun, the moon, and the stars. But here we are on the first day—and obviously, there is no electricity—so where is this light coming from? It's a light that is coming not from the sun or the moon or the stars. It is not simple illumination. It is something more.

When we look at the original text, the answer becomes even more clear, because the Hebrew word used to denote light in this passage is *ohr*. And when we consider how the word *ohr* is used in other places in the Bible, we begin to understand that it doesn't mean an ordinary light, but a supernatural light. I would call it a "life force," specifically a divine life force.

So the first thing God created was life.

This life didn't take on the character of any being at first—not an insect, not an animal, not a human. It was a metaphysical, divine life energy that permeated the whole world. So there was only one thing that existed before the world was created, and that was darkness, which is a form of death. The first act of creation brought into being its opposite—life. The life force. This ancient passage is telling us from its very opening lines that this is the way of the world. There will always be darkness and chaos and confusion. We will feel the void of death all around us and lapse into despair. But the Bible is also saying that if we want to help one another we must—like God—bring the light of our life force to that darkness.

The French philosopher Henri Bergson coined a nice phrase for this. He called it *élan vital*. In English we often translate this as "creative force," but we might also read it as "vital energy." And energy—if we remember the laws of physics—can never be destroyed; it can only be transformed.

That is exactly what I'm talking about here—we are healthy or sick to the extent that we transform this vital energy into a creative force in our lives.

ONE OF MY PATIENTS, WHO SUFFERS FROM SLEEPLESSNESS AS A RESULT of many emotional and physical problems, described to me quite poignantly the intolerable oppression of her insomnia. In so doing, she helped me understand the key difference between ordinary external light and the internal life force. She said, "I wake up at 12:15 and there is darkness. I wake up at 1:30 and there is darkness. I wake up at 2:45 and there is darkness. And finally, even when dawn comes, I don't feel the light."

Obviously, when dawn comes there is sunlight, but she is so depressed, in such personal darkness, that she can hardly move. She has no energy; she cannot *feel* the light. She feels no creative energy driving her forward. She is absorbed in herself, in her process of illness, in her fear of death. In that darkness and despair, she cannot bring her creative force to bear.

In such moments of darkness, it is very difficult to recognize that you are capable of anything else. It is hard to realize that you may need to go through darkness in order to learn that you, too, are a creator and can create "light." But it is also true that even in the worst of times, there is a way of connecting to the life force within you that God gave the world that first day. It is possible to be the creator of your own heaven, just as it is possible to be the creator of your own hell.

The life force is not something "out there." It is within you, and it is possible to bring it into any situation and transform that situation by creative action. As I said, this process is extremely difficult. And it takes time, patience, and endurance.

How do you begin?

There are two approaches. One is symbolic—because symbols can be very powerful and have a creative and healing energy of their own—and the other is through specific, concrete actions.

One of my rabbinical students took it upon himself as a special project to offer Sabbath candles to all the patients in my hospital. He understood that candlelight represents the life force, and to light a candle in the room of a sick person is a life-affirming act. These patients are mostly in contact with the death force, the destructiveness of illness. While lighting candles is a symbolic act, it can have concrete positive consequences. For example, several nurses have reported to me that quite often, after a candle has been lit, the sickest of patients appear to be calmer and enjoy a few hours of respite from pain.

I am also reminded of a particular patient, an elderly Romanian Jew, whom I encountered early in my chaplaincy career. He was gravely ill and had decided to be listed as "no code," meaning he did not desire high-tech interventions that might extend his life. But despite that decision, as death neared, he asked to be placed on a ventilator that would assist him with his breathing.

The hospital personnel, feeling his request was a panic reaction to approaching death, were reluctant to prolong this harrowing process, and they asked me to talk him out of it. But while speaking with him, I felt something more was going on, and as a result of my intervention, the patient was placed on a ventilator. To everyone's amazement, he felt much better after a few days and asked to be taken down to the chapel.

As it happened, this was the first day of Chanukah, and he participated in the special candlelighting ceremony that is such an important part of the Festival of Lights. Only then did I realize the meaning of everything that had happened. This man, as he neared death, needed to connect with the light, and he knew somewhere in the depths of his being that he would have to hold out until Chanukah to do so.

He died in peace.

IN A HOSPITAL EVERYTHING IS SCIENTIFIC. AND IT'S GOOD THAT IT IS. Science helps a lot of people, but everyone who works in a hospital knows that sometimes there is a magic in the healing process that science can't explain. Supernatural things occur that defy scientific understanding. Patients awaken from comas despite their physicians' most dire prognoses. Cancers mysteriously disappear, and those told they have a year left to live somehow manage to survive ten.

If you recognize the presence of the supernatural and don't just dismiss it as "one of those unexplainable things," you begin to see that this *ohr,* this life force, is not something *outside* you but something *within* you. And if you connect with it, you can transform yourself and others.

I grant you, it's extremely hard to do, particularly when you are in the midst of difficult, desperate times. I know a woman who suffers from ovarian cancer; she has had three surgeries and several biopsies, all of which have indicated that the cancer is still present. She is in despair. How can she connect to her life force? How can she have a life?

I have no formulas, no easy answers for such a person. That is real darkness. That is reality, so poetically described in the open ing passage of Genesis. Yet I know that, as God created light, we, too, must create light from this chaotic darkness. And I have confidence that this woman will.

I have watched as over the course of her illness she has begun to change her outlook and priorities. She used to be totally absorbed by the concerns of her immediate family, but now she is talking of becoming a nurse in order to serve the human family, to ease the pain of strangers.

Her reaction is not uncommon. People have often spoken to me about how their priorities have shifted in the face of serious or terminal illness. Like the character played by Clint Eastwood in the movie *Unforgiven*—who, after recovering from near-fatal wounds, remarks that only now that he has come so close to death does he see the beauty of the countryside around him—they see with different eyes. Suddenly, promotions seem meaningless, endless hours spent at the office at the expense of a close-knit family a waste of time, material possessions inconsequential. Endless questions haunt them: What have I missed? Have I been the best person I could have been? Have I been too busy to listen to a friend in trouble? Have I allowed the banal and the trivial to divert me from the all-important task of using my vital energy to help create light in the world?

Viktor Frankl, the famed psychiatrist and author of *Man's Search for Meaning,* shared with me the story of a patient he treated, a young woman who, at age nineteen, could only complain about the meaninglessness of her life. Ironically, only after she was injured in a motorcycle accident did she begin to look at life in a new way. As she was a quadriplegic, her physical abilities were severely limited, but her capacities to think and feel were enhanced. As this young woman became more alive to the world both outside and within her, she discovered a new meaning and purpose.

It is sad that we reach for the light only when it is gone or when its presence is threatened. It is much, much easier to start before a tragedy occurs.

There are many ways—small, everyday ways—in which we can bring the light of the life force into our world. For a start, we might begin by allowing ourselves to be more open. We can admit our vulnerabilities to those we love and be less guarded and more honest in our intimate conversations. We can be more supportive and encouraging of our friends and coworkers. When you do so, you bring life affirmation to those people. On the other hand, if you are constantly criticizing, you are acting contrary to life affirmation. If this sounds cryptic, consider what it means when someone comes to you with a new idea and you respond, "Yes, but . . ." Are you a person who always says, "Yes, but . . ."? If so, you may be acting in a way that is opposite to life affirmation by always finding reasons to put a damper on creative ideas.

To the extent that you are a life-affirming person, you have the capacity to connect with not only the life force that dwells within you but the life force that dwells within others and the life force that dwells outside all of us.

This is a deep idea and another level at which the opening lines of the Bible are to be understood. You may have asked yourself, "Why is God creating *ohr*?" That's a valid question. What is the purpose?

This is the first thing He creates, so apparently it is something that He wants to be part of the creative process, part of the scheme of things. I mean, why not just start with the sun and moon and stars?

God gives us the creative force first, because He intends for humanity to be cocreators with Him and continue the process of bringing light to the universe.

It's a powerful idea. Having been given this life force, we can nurture it or corrupt it—this is the key to living in light or living in darkness.

So ask yourself: Are you working to give back what you have been given? Are you giving it to others around you? If you are, you are also giving it back to God.

2

The Union of Opposites

S WE READ ABOUT THE LIGHT AND THE REST OF THE creation story, it is easy to miss the nuances that are there.

After everything has been created, God proclaims that it is all "very good." But suddenly, something is amiss; something is "not good." Shortly after God creates man, He declares, *"It is not good for man to be alone."*

To fix the problem, God decides to create a helpmate for Adam. Here is another place where one of those easy-to-miss nuances slips in. The exact words that God chooses to use are puzzling. He says, *"I will make a helpmate against him."*

This is an unusual choice of words to describe someone who is supposed to be a helpmate. It's not good for man to be alone, so let's give him a helpmate who'll be *against* him? Some helper!

But really, what the Bible is saying here is that this helpmate will be the *opposite* of Adam. She won't be his clone. She won't think exactly as he does and always say, "Yes, you're so right,

Adam. . . . You took the words right out of my mouth." No, she'll be someone who is different, who thinks differently, and who has a different perspective on life. She will say, "Adam, you may not have considered the other side of the argument."

But at the same time, she is to be his *helpmate,* which is to say, she is not there to make his life miserable—she is not there to criticize him all the time or nag him to death. She is there to make his life interesting, as he is there to make her life interesting; their joint task is to tend the Garden of Eden, to take care of the trees and the animals. To put it simply, they exist for the betterment of each other and the world.

The story of the creation of man and woman ends with the following sentence: *"Hence a man shall leave his father and mother and cling to his wife, so that they become one flesh."*

It is interesting that the Bible makes this point here. Because clearly, Adam and Eve did not have parents. The Bible is speaking for the future of humankind. It is saying that God made man and woman for a reason, and that reason is that they should leave their families and form a separate family unit.

In twentieth century psychology, we put a great deal of emphasis on the concept of "individuation." That is, it is important to the maturation of a human being that he or she separate from the mother or father complex that might be present. Yet what happens in our society so often? People marry duplicates of their parents.

I have one client who, when he wants to refer to his wife, often says "my mother." Freudian slip. Very funny. But it is not funny at all, because this man, who is past middle age already, is stuck in some sort of child-parent relationship with his wife. Although he is successful in business, his wife manages all his money and he gets an allowance from her every week.

It is precisely this kind of pattern that the Bible is warning us against: God created a helpmate for you so that you could *leave* your parents, not re-create them in your marriage.

The other key aspect of that biblical sentence is the last phrase: *"so that they become one flesh."*

Notice the word "flesh." It does not say, "so they could become one soul."

I want to emphasize this point, because of late there has been much misunderstanding of the concept of having a soul mate—so much that I sometimes wish people would stop using the word.

A client recently came to see me, very concerned because somehow he'd gotten the idea that he is supposed to find his soul mate—one person out there who is his other half and without whom he cannot have a whole soul. And he asked me how one goes about finding that person.

I assured him that his soul actually yearns to achieve completeness with the universe and with God, but such completeness is impossible to achieve with any one human being. I also told him that the Bible instructs us that it is important to find a mate—someone who will be a helper in this process of uniting with the larger whole of which we are all a part—but that no one person can provide all the missing pieces.

If he makes the mistake of believing that it is possible to find one person who will be the whole universe for him, he will most certainly end up disappointed. And it is my opinion that people who marry under this impression soon begin to look outside their marriage for satisfaction; often they divorce, only to begin again the process of looking for that singular individual who does not exist.

IT HAS BEEN SAID THAT ALTHOUGH IT IS IMPORTANT TO FIND THE right person, it is more important to *become* the right person.

If you are fortunate enough to find someone who wants to help you become the right person, believe me, you have also been fortunate enough to find the right helpmate.

A helpmate is a positive catalyst. He or she knows how to listen to you and advise you, putting personal, selfish interests aside. He or she knows how to create a loving atmosphere in which you can flourish creatively and intellectually, passionately and spiritually. (Indeed, psychiatrist and author M. Scott Peck, in the perennial favorite *The Road Less Traveled,* defined love as the concern for the spiritual growth of another.)

But even if you are fortunate enough to find such a helpmate, it cannot be assumed that everything will go smoothly for you from that moment on. Both of you will sometimes stumble and fall. Here, it is instructive to remember what happened to Adam and his helpmate, Eve.

So let us now return to the story of Paradise. Not everyone who is familiar with the story knows that there were two important trees in the Garden of Eden—the tree of life and the tree of knowledge of good and evil.

Adam and Eve were free to eat of the tree of life, but the other tree was off limits. God told Adam, *"Of every tree of the garden you are free to eat; but as for the tree of knowledge of good and evil, you must not eat of it; for on the day that you eat of it, you shall die."* So one is the tree of life, while the other is the tree of death.

Note that both trees were created by God, as was the serpent, who is about to make his entry onto the stage of human history. He has a big part to play, yet he speaks scarcely two lines in this drama. However, what he says matters not so much as what Adam and Eve do in response to his temptation. But since God created everything—the good and the evil, the serpent and the temptation—can Adam and Eve be responsible for what they do? This is one of the secrets of life we are trying to unlock in this book.

Remember, humanity was created with free will. But free will would be meaningless—it would not *be* free will—if humankind were not free to make choices. So now God provides Adam and Eve with a situation in which they can exercise their free will and make a choice. They have the opportunity to choose to obey God or not, with the consequences clearly delineated.

Notice that this is early in the story of humankind, and the first human beings have only one commandment to obey—not seven commandments as Noah gets, not ten as Moses gets, not 613 as the Israelites later get. Only one—not to eat of the tree of knowledge of good and evil. And this one little commandment turns out to be one too many. They can't abide by it, even though the consequences have been made clear—and are dire.

Notice that Adam and Eve do not have *any* excuse for breaking this one law. Today, when we violate a commandment, we may say, "Well, I was pushed in this direction because I was in emotional pain. If you only knew what my childhood was like, if you only knew how my mother treated me, you'd understand why I have tasted the forbidden fruit."

Adam and Eve could not use that excuse. They had no worries about earning a living, no worries about food, and no worries about their children, since they did not yet have any. But they could resort to the other less-than-admirable behavior to which people resort when they violate a commandment or, for that matter, break any rule in society: They spread the blame.

As soon as she ate, Eve gave the fruit to her husband, and he ate as well. Incidentally, a lot of people think it was an apple. But the Bible does not identify what kind of fruit it was; it says only "fruit." The apple is actually a Western notion; in the Middle East, where apples were unknown until relatively recent times, tradition holds it to be a fig or grape. Whatever it was, they both ate it, and in quick succession.

But when caught by God, neither wants to accept the blame. Adam says, *"She gave me of the tree . . ."* Eve says, *"The serpent enticed me."*

Isn't this the same thing that happens all the time in the modern world? When a person has done something he is ashamed of, what happens? He seeks to displace the responsibility. It's always something else or someone else that is responsible. It's never "Yes, I have done something wrong." It's always "Him . . . over there . . . the serpent."

But Adam and Eve do feel guilty, and their guilt is manifested in a very interesting way. Suddenly, *"the eyes of both of them were opened and they perceived that they were naked."*

Only seven sentences before that, we were told, *"the two of them were naked . . . yet they felt no shame."* The difference is that before they sinned, Adam and Eve had an innocence about them and their nakedness had no unseemly connotations. But after they committed a transgression, they felt exposed, and their innocence changed to guilt. Nakedness is the symbol of guilt.

The Danish writer Jens Peter Jacobsen illustrates this beautifully in his masterful novel *Niels Lyhne.* A female character in the novel has an extramarital affair of great depth and passion with Niels. But when she learns that her husband has died in a tragic accident, her eyes are opened and her "sacred relationship" now appears as a cheap, regrettable liaison.

Filled with guilt, she feels naked, as she tells Niels: "Day after day I will have to live with this stigma on my soul, and never will I meet anyone so degraded that I won't know in my heart that I am even more degraded."

Few people, when ridden with guilt, have such depth of insight. Most people do the more expedient thing—and like Adam and Eve, who immediately started sewing fig leaves into loincloths—they try to cover up.

But even for Adam and Eve, the fig leaves were not enough. They couldn't cover themselves enough. They still felt exposed. And when they heard God coming, they hid. Could they hide from God? Obviously not. Can we hide from our conscience? Ultimately not. Because what happened in the Garden of Eden does repeat itself in the modern world, no matter how much we too might want to escape into the bushes.

It is important to remember that in the story God comes closer, then asks Adam a question: *"Where are you?"* We all understand that God knows where Adam is and what he has done. We all know that God doesn't need to ask where Adam is hiding. But He asks anyway, *"Where are you?"*

God wants Adam to consider this question for himself. What have you done to yourself? Who have you become? Where are you now? Thus we learn that the stories and symbols of the Bible are like blueprints for all of human life—for the constant dilemmas and struggles that confront us. Here is a question we are forced to ask ourselves consciously or unconsciously all the time: Where are you in your life? You have married well, you have lovely children, a wealth of material possessions. Where are you? Or you have divorced, your oldest son is on drugs, you can't pay the second mortgage. Where are you? And, most important, where are you in terms of your relationship with God?

When God asks this question of Adam and Eve, they have no answers. Their crude attempts to divert the blame would make anyone wince, and they make God angry. So Adam and Eve must take the consequences of which they were clearly warned. They must now follow the path they chose for themselves: They were told that if they ate of the tree of knowledge of good and evil, they would die. They chose the tree of death, and thus they chose the tortuous path of mortality. So Adam and Eve, and all of humanity to come, were banished from the Garden of Eden, with the way back to the tree of life guarded by cherubim wielding fiery swords.

Outside the garden lies the world as we know it—a world where pain and suffering are the teachers, where mortality dwells. This is the choice the first man and woman made for us—they chose to have knowledge of good and evil, to have consciousness, at the price of death. And it is interesting to see where that consciousness leads them. Right away, Adam and Eve have children—two sons. So there are now four people on earth, and what happens? Cain chooses evil and murders his good brother, Abel. Then he has the insolence to say to God, who asks what happened to Abel, *"Am I my brother's keeper?"* These words of the Bible echo to us through time.

If we are not our brother's keeper, if we are not concerned with what happens around us—in our neighborhood, our city, the world—who are we? Are we not like Cain? Everything we do is about the choice between good and evil, the choice between life and death.

This is the key lesson of the Five Books of Moses, the core of the Bible. Later, Moses drives this point home most poignantly in his farewell address to his people: *"I call heaven and earth to witness against you this day: I have put before you life and death, blessing and curse. . . . Choose life!"* He seems to be saying: Correct the mistake of Adam and Eve. Choose life. We need not be banished forever. But how does one choose life? There is a way.

When God banished Adam and Eve, He did not abandon them. He continued to follow them, guide them, and speak to them, although, as we know, they—and many of their descendants—chose to ignore His voice. But then there came a truly unique human being whom we all know today by the name of Abraham. It is his story—and what he teaches us about hearing the voice of God within us—that we shall take up next.

3

—

The Voice Within

STATISTICIANS TELL US THAT AMERICANS CHANGE CAREERS approximately three times during their lives. Some of this flux can, of course, be explained by the demands of changing technology and the fast pace of the modern world, but a more interesting phenomenon is also at work, particularly among baby boomers. And it seems to happen most commonly among people between the ages of thirty and forty-five. In that age bracket there seem to be a substantial number of people who, after being highly successful in a given profession, decide to start over and try something totally different. This is happening with greater and greater frequency. A successful computer analyst working for Dow Jones leaves his career to become a writer. An opera diva decides, at age thirty-two, to enter medical school and become a gynecologist. A parole officer becomes a newspaper reporter. A newspaper reporter becomes an airline pilot. A businessperson becomes a rabbi.

All of the above examples are of real people. More often than not, such a dramatic change is accompanied by an equally dramatic cut in salary, because the person has to start at the bottom again. Yet these people don't seem to mind; they sell their BMWs and their vacation homes because they are so driven to do something else.

I asked one such person—who quit a high-paying, secure job with the federal government to begin a career in news reporting—why she had done it. She groped for words. She had not been really unhappy in her government job, although it had lost its challenge. She'd had to start from the bottom in her new career, taking a part-time job and doing many mundane tasks. She'd known the rewards at the outset would be few. She'd known she wasn't going to change the world and would be making a fraction of her former salary. So what had the appeal been? Finally she said, "Something inside me said I had to do it. And this feeling was so strong, it drove me on. I didn't calculate my chances for success. . . . I just had to do it."

As it happened, this woman went on from that first part-time job to do some significant work as a newspaper reporter and was even nominated for a Pulitzer Prize. But it started with "Something inside me said I had to do it."

Now, I tell this story because in some ways it is a modern version of what we see happen to Abram (who later is renamed Abraham) in the Bible. He gets a call. God tells him to do something else—to take on a new career, if you will. God says, *"Go forth from your native land, from your birthplace, and from your father's house to the land that I will show you."*

A lot of people who read this passage assume that God was speaking with a booming voice from heaven, loud and clear, as if through a megaphone, and that Abram had no trouble hearing it. They assume he knew it was God speaking, and therefore he obeyed. But it has been my experience that God doesn't work that way. I don't think that's how it happened.

In *Abraham,* a recent television version of the story, God's voice is portrayed as Abram's own voice. This was very perceptive on the part of the filmmakers. Because what Abram most certainly heard was an inner voice, something inside him. And the inner voice is a silent voice.

Abram heard that voice on many occasions during his lifetime, as the Bible recounts, but here we are concerned with the first time he heard it, what I will refer to as "the initiation call."

An initiation call is when you hear an inner voice that you feel is a higher voice, a divine voice that tells you to redirect your life in a certain way. Of course, most people resist the call. The Bible is replete with instances of resistance—Moses resists, Jonah resists. Jonah even wants to flee! Because to respond to the call means to accept a mission, and the mission can seem awesome. So the normal response is to resist.

We all hear the call many times throughout our lives, but for most of us it is drowned out by so many competing voices that are not inner voices but really outer voices, the voices of our ego. This is why Abram is such an exemplary role model. Because he hears the call and goes.

I would venture to say that Abram had a tremendous amount of courage. What he was asked to do was no small thing. How many people, if they heard an inner voice, would leave their country, their birthplace, and their father's house? On the basis of a promise, no less. Does God show him the land? No. He just makes a promise that eventually Abram will be shown the land.

So Abram is asked to leave everything familiar and go to an unknown place. Now, what feeling immediately surfaces when something is unknown? Fear. I don't want to go there; I want to make sure it's at least got a Hilton. I want to know that I'll be taken care of and protected. Are you going to pay my bill? Let it be a nice place. Is it going to be a land flowing with milk and honey, or will there be a lot of giants? Will I be safe there? But Abram doesn't ask these questions. He just goes.

I am reminded of a visit I made nine years ago to a patient on his deathbed. It just happened to be the time of year when this section of the Bible is read. So I read this part of the story to him at his bedside, and he said to me, "This voice which speaks to Abram is the voice that I'm experiencing right now, because I am going to a land that God will show me. I don't know what it will be like. The way that Abram listened is the same way that I will listen."

Very few individuals are that aware. But that is the essence of religious belief; that the message of the Bible can be a *living* force, one that you can apply to your own situation.

WHAT ARE THE REWARDS? THE BIBLE TELLS US THAT GOD SAID TO Abram, *"I will make of you a great nation. . . . I will make your name great, and you shall be a blessing."*

That's quite a promise!

If you follow the call of initiation, whatever you do will be a blessing for yourself, for the people around you, for your family, for your country, and for all of humanity. You *shall* be a blessing.

This should give us a great deal of hope. Because the Bible is saying that if you respond to the initiation call and move forward, after that, whatever decision you make, you literally cannot go wrong. That's a pretty attractive proposition. Yet when most people hear that inner voice, that initiation call, they say, "Yes, but . . ." "Yes, but I have to set all the parameters. I can't look at what's good for humanity. I can only look at what's good for me and my family."

That is not responding to the call. That is not being a blessing. Being a blessing means that every aspect of who you are and what you do makes you a role model for other people.

The Hebrew word for "blessing" is *bracha*, which happens to be related to *braycha*, meaning "spring of water." Tradition suggests that if you act in a certain way, you will be like a spring of water, allowing divine energies to flow through you. In other words, you are to *conduct* yourself in such a way that you will be a *conduit* for divine energies.

This is what it means to be a blessing.

THIS ANCIENT DOCUMENT IS GIVING US THREE POWERFUL LESSONS for use in the modern world.

First, that you will hear an initiation call that will begin your process of becoming and realizing your best self.

Second, that there will definitely be pain and struggle involved because you will have to separate and differentiate yourself from your parents, from your birthplace, from your milieu. You will have to go to an unknown place, which will fill you with a feeling of insecurity.

Everyone wants security, but nothing can really make us secure, because life itself is a journey into the unknown. Insecurity is at the core of life. Throughout our lives, we try to make ourselves secure, sometimes with real things and sometimes with things that exist only in fantasy. But ultimately, we all go to a land we do not know.

The third lesson is that the work is hard, scary—even terrifying at times—but the rewards are great. As God tells Abram, *"I will make your name great, and you shall be a blessing."* And later on: *"Look toward heaven and count the stars, if you are able to count them. . . . So shall your offspring be."*

God tells a childless man—who is very old at this point in the story and who has a barren wife and therefore seemingly no hope of having children—that his descendants will be too many to count. Yet Abram believes God, and that promise is fulfilled.

But the question is, When God makes that promise, why does He tell Abram to look up at the stars? What is the deeper meaning here? Simply that God wants Abram to be in touch with what is infinite. You, also, must learn to look and observe the part of your life that is beyond you, to look at the infinite. So finally, we are told that being in touch with the voice inside of us is part and parcel of a much greater whole—making a connection with the beyond, being in touch with the stars, being in touch with the infinite, being in touch with God.

4

Talking Back to God

SOMETIMES, READING THE STORY OF HUMANITY'S BEHAVIOR in the Bible feels like sitting on a seesaw. It's good followed by evil, kindness followed by cruelty, love followed by hate. Before long you begin to discern that one balances the other, that the undulating rhythm of human progress through time would be impossible without both, just as the movement of a seesaw would be impossible without two weights.

So we get the beautiful, idyllic Garden of Eden. But then we get the snake and the expulsion from Paradise.

We get Abel. But then we get Cain.

We get Noah. But then comes the Tower of Babel.

We get Abraham, the most righteous man of his time. But then come the cities of Sodom and Gomorrah, where sin and perversion abound. These two cities—and God's plan to destroy them—provide a supreme challenge to our biblical hero.

Abraham knows that good people do live in Sodom, among

them his nephew Lot and Lot's family, and he realizes that they, too, will be destroyed. To Abraham, it seems a great injustice that the good should be destroyed along with the evil. So Abraham dares to question God. He asks—and his tone of incredulity is apparent from his very words, *"Will You sweep away the innocent along with the guilty? What if there should be fifty innocent within the city; will You then wipe out the place and not forgive it for the sake of the innocent fifty who are in it?"*

Thus far, Abraham has been most submissive to the will of God. When God first called him, he said "Yes" without qualification. He left the house of his father, breaking with his family; he made the covenant with God, knowing that this great honor would also bring great suffering to his descendants; he allowed himself (at a time when no anesthetics existed) to be circumcised at the age of ninety-nine. (Later, as we all know, he is willing to offer his beloved son, Isaac, as a sacrifice, obeying a command from God.)

It seems that it was in Abraham's nature to be submissive, that he was an innately gentle, humble man, always welcoming strangers and attracting a considerable following through his kindness and generous heart. But now he is put into a position where he is about to see such a grave injustice done that he must do what does not come naturally to him: speak out against it.

And this gentle man becomes angry with God. He actually accuses God, saying, *"Far be it from You to do such a thing, to bring death upon the innocent as well as the guilty, so that innocent and guilty fare alike. Far be it from You! Shall not the Judge of all the earth deal justly?"*

Thus he calls God to account—not submitting, not wringing his hands, not dismissing what is about to happen as the "Will of the Almighty" but arguing, questioning God's intentions, demanding justice. And he wins the argument.

God concedes that Abraham is right. The cities will not be destroyed even if there are only ten good inhabitants. Amazing, isn't it? The Bible is actually saying you can argue with God and prevail.

This story teaches us two important lessons: first, that our greatest challenges are apt to demand something from us that is not natural, not easy; and second—and most important—that our relationship with God is one not of silent submission but of dialogue.

We already showed in Chapter 1 that it is our obligation to create light from darkness, much as God created light in the beginning of the world. Here we develop this idea of cocreation further. Abraham teaches us that a meaningful relationship with God is a partnership. We are allowed to question, to speak up, and God pays attention.

It is important to note that Abraham was a person of great faith. You cannot live your life according to your own rules and then, when things go wrong, accuse God of unfairness. But if, like Abraham, you live a life of faith, you are allowed to question. And you are not only allowed to question; you are *mandated* to question. So go ahead, speak up!

Yet many religious people are afraid to do so. Their upbringing has sometimes done them a disservice by teaching them to fear God, thus inhibiting them from speaking back to someone so terrifying. They would feel much closer to God if they understood "fear" as "awe" which would allow for respectful dialogue and questioning.

I am reminded of a patient at whose bedside I spent some time while he awaited a liver transplant. He was a middle-aged man, very sweet and gentle, in the way Abraham might have been. He was most grateful for my visits, always thanking me profusely. Then one day, as I was about to leave his room, he said with tears in his eyes, "You know, the most difficult thing for me to do is pray. I don't know how to pray. . . . I've never learned any prayers."

I went over to him, took his hand, and said, "Let me say a prayer with you. I pray that the next time we meet, you can find just a few words to say to God."

He did. And in so doing, he realized that praying is a dialogue. It is talking with God. He had thought of prayer as a recitation of a lot of memorized verses; he had thought of praying as a form of begging. He did not know—because he had never been taught—that praying is talking to God.

I encounter many people who have this kind of attitude. Another patient who comes to mind is a religious woman who spends every Saturday morning in the synagogue. She can recite a hundred prayers by heart. But when I encountered her in the hospital, this woman asked me, "Why am I suffering?"

"Ask God," I suggested. "Include this question in your prayers."

She seemed surprised at the suggestion. "But will I actually hear God's answer?"

When I explained to her that of course she would hear the answer—with her inner ear—she stared at me in disbelief. Although she had prayed all her life, the idea that prayer was a dialogue—not a monologue—was foreign to her.

So I cannot stress this point enough: *Prayer is a conversation with God.* Sometimes we express gratitude; sometimes we ask questions; sometimes we argue; sometimes we just share. A person who has this kind of relationship with God is likely to relate to the world at large in the same manner.

After I discussed this idea during a lecture in my Bible class, one of the participants, a young woman I'll call "Mary," approached me. She said she had been raised in a Catholic home and had not been previously aware that the Bible taught this lesson, but she said, "I learned it from my grandmother." She then proceeded to tell me this story.

As a ten-year-old child, Mary was caught by a policeman while playing on the railroad tracks. The policeman—intending, no doubt, to scare her enough that she would never do such a dangerous thing again—threatened her with jail. Mary believed him and was so distraught that she began to sob, pleading for mercy. In her despair, she knelt down on the ground, begging him to let her go. Having made his point, he did.

By the time she got home, a neighbor had informed her grandmother of what had happened. Mary's grandmother was very angry—not because Mary had been playing on the railroad tracks and could have been killed, but because she had knelt down before the policeman. "Remember this, and never forget it," her grandmother said. "Never kneel before any man. Never. No matter who he is, no matter what position of authority he holds. You only kneel before God, and even about that you should think twice."

Mary said she had never forgotten what her grandmother had said. Later in life, she had had to face some very difficult moments, such as when she had had to challenge a white supervisor's racist attitude toward black employees. She felt that her grandmother's advice had helped her find the courage to speak up.

Inadvertently, Mary had also learned another lesson that derives from this one—that it is our obligation to speak up in the face of injustice or evil, no matter how mighty the opposition might be, no matter if the opposition is God Himself, because an injustice may take place simply because people stand by idly and do nothing.

I learned of just such a case through another therapist. He had a woman client who was going through a difficult time while deciding whether to divorce her husband, an anesthesiologist who had become addicted to the drugs he administered in the operating room. What troubled this woman, as well as her therapist, was that the anesthesiologist worked daily with people who must have been aware that he had a drug problem; it was evident from his slurred speech and vacant stare. Yet no one had spoken up. The many nurses and surgeons with whom he came into contact had just minded their own business. His wife feared that no one would act to prevent him from continuing to treat patients until a tragedy occurred.

Tragedies occur all too frequently because people find it too hard to get involved with all the issues that such action entails. But "I should have" is meaningless after a person dies or is irreparably harmed. It is just this kind of behavior that has led to the vast changes in the laws surrounding child abuse. In one case I shall never forget, a boy of eight was so brutally and systematically beaten by his mother over a period of years that when he finally died, the coroner was at a loss to find the one injury that had caused his death. He had serious injuries to his kidneys and liver, internal hemorrhaging, broken bones—old and new—and skull fractures.

He had been seen by school nurses, teachers, neighbors, and social workers and had been treated in various emergency rooms on several occasions. Yet the soul searching did not begin until after he died. That case happened a number of years ago, and fortunately, we now have laws mandating the reporting of suspected child abuse, with penalties attached for health professionals who fail to do so. These laws were passed simply because such professionals had, for too long, minded their own business.

Another group of professionals that has come under scrutiny of late is my own—psychotherapists. Statistics indicate that as many as 10 percent of licensed therapists have been involved in sexual impropriety with their clients. This is a particularly heinous offense, since the client, who is putting all of his or her trust in the therapist, is emotionally very vulnerable and can be easily manipulated sexually. When such an affair later falls apart—which happens more often than not—the damage to the client is irreparable. How can this person, who obviously needs help more than ever, now open up to another therapist? Moreover, it is especially difficult for a client to make such an accusation in a public forum. Yet some people have had the courage to do so, which is why we are becoming aware of the seriousness of this problem and are taking steps to rectify it.

Another example. A recent issue of the *Los Angeles Times Magazine* graphically described the persecution of foreign laborers in Germany over the course of the last few years. In one incident, a group of young neo-Nazi thugs threw a firebomb into the home of a Turkish family. The family had been sleeping, and by the time the parents managed to get all the children out, they were badly burned.

The parents were screaming for help in the street, trying to cope with the terrible injuries of their children. No one came to help them. People looked out to see what was going on, but not one soul went over to offer aid or comfort.

Now, I would expect that all these lookers-on pay their taxes on time, mow their lawns, put out the garbage, and obey the law. If you asked each one of them about himself or herself, he or she would claim to be a good person. And yet . . .

Subsequently, I was heartened to see a CNN report that showed thousands of Germans demonstrating against such incidents. The demonstrators were people who wanted to stand up and be counted, to speak up and be heard, and, in so doing, to stop evil in its tracks.

While we can all cite examples we've read in the newspapers— of harm done because people minded their own business— opportunities to speak up arise for us all quite frequently.

The most obvious example of taking responsibility is not allowing a friend—or even a stranger—to drive drunk. It can take real strength of character, even courage, to risk a friendship when someone does not want to be persuaded. It is so much easier to mind your own business. Yet it is out of seemingly simple, everyday acts such as this that the strength to tackle much greater challenges is born. This strength does not spring up overnight; it is nurtured little by little. And when the time comes, we are ready to battle the worst of evils because we have been getting into shape for it little by little—by voting, speaking up when need be, minding our community's and our country's business, and, as partners with God, keeping up a dialogue with Him that enables us to face all the challenges we encounter.

5

—

Truth or Consequences

PERHAPS THE GREATEST AND MOST COMPLEX MORAL LESSONS we find in the Bible are contained in the chapters dealing with Jacob, the son of Isaac. Jacob, more than any other biblical personality, struggles from his birth to his death with questions that trouble humanity to this day. In fact, his struggle begins even *before* he is born—in his mother's womb.

While Rebecca, Isaac's wife, is pregnant with Jacob, she is greatly troubled by what she is experiencing within her body. She is not just feeling the discomfort that might accompany a baby's normal kicking; a painful wrestling match seems to be going on, and she is afraid of what this might mean for her future child. So Rebecca does the only thing she can—she prays. The answer comes straight from God: She is carrying twins, who represent two separate warring nations, and even more significantly, *"the older shall serve the younger."*

Shortly thereafter, she does indeed give birth to two boys. The first boy to emerge will develop into the hairy, hot-tempered, impulsive Esau. Second, clutching Esau's heel, comes his twin, who will develop into the wholesome, mild-mannered, God-loving Jacob.

It is essential to note that, as twins, these boys are the product of a single impregnation. The Bible is using the metaphor of twins to teach us that the opposing forces of good and evil exist within every individual. Each of us embodies these twin personalities. We are each partially Jacob and partially Esau. Even the best among us, who might be mostly Jacob, still contain some Esau, just as the Esaus of this world are never totally evil; they too have some good in them. This is one of the great paradoxes of life, and the story of Jacob and Esau sheds light on many complicated aspects of human nature.

In this day and age of "the public's right to know," we are learning more and more about the less-than-admirable qualities of the great luminaries of our age. For example, we have learned that John F. Kennedy, one of the most beloved American presidents of our time, was unfaithful to his wife and sometimes even cruel in his indiscretions. On the other hand, we have also learned that serial killer Jeffrey Dahmer was, as a rule, "pleasant, polite, free of prejudice, and gentle," according to the state of Wisconsin forensic psychiatrist who examined him. The story of Jacob and Esau illustrates the necessity of recognizing and coming to terms with the opposing forces within us. If we deny that we have a dark side, we deceive ourselves and only complicate the struggle. The only way to accept our shadow is to discover the purpose of our evil inclination and to find a way for it to serve the development of the good inclination within us.

Gershom Scholem, the well-known interpreter of the mystical writings of the Kabbala, teaches that evil wins out only when it becomes separated and isolated. When it exists in balance with goodness, it serves the greater development of the good—as God tells Rebecca, Esau will someday *serve* Jacob. But neither Rebecca nor her son Jacob (under her influence) allows God to fulfill this prophecy. Instead, they adopt the well-known attitude of "the end justifies the means" and take matters into their own hands.

The story is told that, one day, Esau comes home "starving" at the very moment Jacob is cooking some lentil soup. Esau demands some food, but Jacob will give it to him only for a price. The price, which the famished Esau is more than willing to pay, is his birthright, namely, the rights of the firstborn.

There is more going on here than a hungry man in search of a meal. Tradition tells us that Jacob is involved in a good deed, preparing the soup for his father, Isaac, on the day his grandfather Abraham has died. While Jacob is involved in this act of consolation and comfort, Esau has been out "hunting." Not content with killing wild animals, Esau has also engaged in other types of predatory behavior. Knowing of Esau's crimes, Jacob has come to the conclusion that his brother cannot be the spiritual heir, the possessor of the birthright and blessing that have been handed down from Abraham to Isaac. But there is also no question that Jacob is preying, in a less-than-admirable way, on his brother's hunger and vulnerability. Perhaps Jacob realizes that this transaction is tainted, because he does not tell his father about it. In due time, the old and nearly blind Isaac, sensing that his death is imminent, decides to confer a blessing on his firstborn, Esau.

While Esau is away, Rebecca convinces the reluctant Jacob to deceive his father in an effort to get the blessing for himself. As the story goes, she covers Jacob's smooth arms with goat hides so that, to Isaac, he feels like hairy Esau, and Jacob receives the blessing.

Again, there is no question that this behavior is devious and unethical; Jacob is again preying on the vulnerability of another— this time, his feeble father. Yet he is ultimately rewarded, becoming the great patriarch whose twelve sons beget the twelve tribes of Israel. How can this be?

First, all the great role models of the Bible are 100 percent human, beset by many faults and vices. What makes them great is their determination to overcome their problems and rise above their baser instincts.

Second, Jacob pays dearly for his lapse of conscience. Although he has the blessing, he hardly has a chance to enjoy it. Esau's wrath is so fierce that Jacob must flee from his home and the people he loves. He goes to the land of his uncle Laban, where he immediately falls in love with his cousin Rachel, who is described in the Bible as *"shapely and beautiful."*

Laban agrees to give him Rachel in marriage in exchange for seven years of work. Jacob loves Rachel so much that he agrees, works hard, and endures the wait, only to find that he has been tricked on his wedding night: Uncle Laban has substituted his older daughter, Leah, the one with the *"tearful eyes,"* for the beautiful Rachel.

To Jacob, this substitution must have brought back some painful memories—the man who tricked his father and brother now experiences what it feels like to be the *victim* of deception. A week later he does get to marry Rachel, but he must work another seven years. Although he gets her at last, there is to be no happiness in the marriage, because Rachel is barren and jealous of the children Leah bears. Leah, on the other hand, is jealous that her sister, Rachel, is Jacob's beloved.

What the Bible is telling us here is that whenever we rationalize that the end justifies the means, we must be prepared to pay the price. Every immoral act requires atonement of some sort in the end. If we deceive, there will be consequences. Occasionally we see no other alternative. However, if we choose to act in an unethical manner to serve a greater good, we must always be aware that, in so doing, we must accept the consequences of what we have done.

I know a couple who, while their daughter was a senior in college, were dismayed to learn that she was dating a lawyer sixteen years her senior. Although they had never met the man, they assumed that the intentions of an older man dating a young girl could not be proper. They reasoned that even if he did intend to marry their daughter, her education would be interrupted and that, furthermore, the age difference was too great for a "good marriage." They spent sleepless nights calculating the impact of this age difference on their future grandchildren and decided that they had to use every means at their disposal—including those crooked and foul—to break up the relationship. Convinced that the end justified the means and that they were preventing their daughter from making a terrible mistake, the parents succeeded in their scheming. The relationship ended.

Today the daughter is forty-three years old and still not married. She has been through a long series of unsuccessful liaisons with a variety of men, including two broken engagements, and her parents have lost hope of ever having any grandchildren. Perhaps they did save their daughter from a terrible mistake, but now they wish they had let her make it.

I will cite another example. For years, one of my clients, "Joyce," had suffered in an emotionally abusive marriage, yet she could not find the strength to break away. Eventually, she "escaped" into an affair with a married man that served as the catalyst she needed to seek a divorce. Shortly afterward, she broke off the adulterous relationship. When, some years later, Joyce met "Ed," a man she very much wanted to marry, she was too ashamed to tell him all the details of her past. Unfortunately, whenever trust is not complete, love suffers, and the little gaps in communication tend to grow larger. Will anyone be surprised to learn that eventually Ed, now Joyce's second husband, betrayed her with another woman?

Joyce ultimately reconciled with Ed, but only after a great deal of anguish and personal struggle. Joyce was not able to forgive her husband until she first came to terms with her own dark side. If *she* had once been capable of adultery, Ed had to be forgiven for the same weakness. I am happy to report that their commitment to each other, with the secrets of the past now out in the open, is stronger than ever.

While this story does have a happy ending, most such situations do not. Yet the pattern of a man or woman being too weak to end a bad marriage is all too common. I have met too many people who have opted for the "safety" of an extramarital affair, which, while solving one problem, creates a whole new set. As Joyce's experience shows, one mistake does not have to doom us forever. Indeed, the paradox of Jacob's story—and the many paradoxes of life— shows us that great good can eventually come from evil. But the price must always be paid.

Eventually Jacob is rewarded, but not until he undergoes an inner transformation. It is this spiritual growth of Jacob through the travails of his exile and his subsequent return from exile to lead his people that we examine next.

6

—

The Lonely Journey

THUS FAR, WE HAVE EXAMINED SOME OF JACOB'S MISTAKES, but we should not forget that Jacob was—with the exception of the two lapses cited—a good and God-loving man who was destined to lead his people.

The process that brought him to the point of readiness for his ultimate destiny was a long, painful journey, and his spiritual struggle offers much guidance for us today.

Let us return to the point in Jacob's story at which he has just deceived his father and must flee from his brother's wrath. This is a dark time in Jacob's life, as he must leave all the people he loves and journey on alone.

Such is the process of transformation; it inevitably happens when we feel the most alone. Often, when some tragedy has befallen us, we feel a deep loneliness. A loved one has betrayed us. A close friend or relative has died. We have committed some wrong, and it seems as if the world has turned against us.

This, of course, is precisely how Jacob feels as he embarks on his lonely journey. Unbeknown to him, when the sun begins to set he has traveled just far enough to reach a significant place. It is no coincidence that he is forced to camp for the night in the same place to which Abraham brought Isaac to offer him as a sacrifice. And this is where Jacob falls asleep, feeling utterly depressed and very much alone.

The Bible tells us that *"he took of the stones of the place, and put them under his head, and lay down in that place to sleep."*

This sentence tells us a great deal. Jacob does not make a comfortable bed for himself; instead, he sleeps on rocks. Surely, even in biblical days, people weren't that hardy. So there's more to this. Jacob's sleeping on rocks underscores his lack of physical comfort at the precise moment when something spiritually transforming is about to take place. Indeed, that is how it is to this day. Spiritual transformations take place more often in the gutter than in a soft bed. Indeed, we are typically not ready for spiritual change until such time as we find ourselves between the so-called rock and a hard place.

I remember well a patient in the emergency room who was strapped to a hard board (used by paramedics to minimize spinal injury) asking, "What have I done that God is punishing me?" I hasten to note that I do not believe that God was "punishing" him, and I told him so, but I found it interesting to discover later that only while lying in a hard place had this man even thought about God. Only then had he been willing to ask a question demanding such self-examination.

Perhaps this is also Jacob's situation. He needs to examine what he has done, but right now he is very lonely and not particularly comfortable lying on rocks. But Jacob does fall asleep on Mount Moriah, and he has a dream. Now, in the Bible, dreams are always very significant, because this is when the spiritual—and often God Himself—speaks most directly and most vividly to human beings.

John A. Sanford, in his book *Dreams: God's Forgotten Language,* says that to this day dreams continue to be one way in which God speaks to us. A number of my clients have confided to me that they've had the sensation, after a particularly vivid dream, that God was trying to tell them something. One man, whom I'll call "Bob," reported having repeatedly had a dream of a taxicab pulling up before him, its door open and waiting. But he had always been afraid to get in. Bob said he had felt as if someone was saying to him over and over, "Hey, don't you get it? This is what I'm telling you." The dream repeated itself until he made some changes in his life—that is, until he got into that taxi and traveled to the next point on his spiritual journey, something he had previously been afraid to do. Of course, we tend to dream in images that are familiar to us, so it is unlikely that Jacob would have dreamt of a taxicab. But he doesn't dream of camels, either. His dream is really quite deep and beautiful.

The Bible tells us that in his dream he sees *"a ladder set up on the ground and its top reached to the sky, and the angels of God were going up and down on it."* Then God appears and tells Jacob, *"And, behold, I am with you, and I will protect you wherever you go and will bring you back to this land; for I will not abandon you until I have done that which I have spoken to you of."*

Jacob wakes up shaken. He realizes that he has stumbled onto a special place imbued with the presence of the divine, and he marks the spot with a stone pillar, intending to return there as God promised in his dream.

The fascinating thing about dreams, both those related in the Bible and those all of us experience just about every night, is that we know we've been dreaming only when we wake up. In the midst of a dream, everything seems just as real as when we are awake.

I propose that it doesn't just *seem* real—it *is* real. That is what the Bible is telling us.

Everyone exists in two realities. Reality one is the state of being awake and alert, the realm of the physical world. Reality two is found in the unconscious, the realm of the psyche. A dream is really a junction, like Jacob's ladder, between divinity and humanity. What is powerful about this image—if you are a spiritual person—is that it helps you recognize that God is with you. So ultimately, you are never alone. The promise God gives to Jacob— *"I will not abandon you"*—is a real promise made to us all.

When Jacob resumes his travels, he does so with a new attitude. The Bible uses an unusual phrase to describe the start of this segment of his journey: *"Then Jacob lifted up his feet."* Why the emphasis on the feet? Why not just say, *"Then Jacob walked on"*?

The famed Bible commentator Rashi explains that once Jacob knew that God was with him, "his heart lifted up his feet and it became easy for him to walk." A revelation: On the spiritual journey, we don't walk with our feet, but with our hearts. Regardless of our physical handicaps or disabilities, we are unlimited in terms of how far we can travel. Indeed, as we already noted, the challenge of a physical handicap can be an asset that provides a person with heightened sensitivity to inner parts of himself or herself. I once counseled a couple, one of whom had a significant physical handicap. Ironically, it was the "disabled" one who was able to help the other find meaning in life beyond the physical plane.

Jacob, too, suffers a physical disability in the course of his journey of transformation, and the Bible presents it as a reminder of a special blessing from God.

After twenty years of working for his uncle Laban, having cleared his debts and accumulated great wealth, Jacob realizes that he will never find inner peace until he reconciles with his brother, Esau. He knows that he must embrace Esau, thus acknowledging the role that the evil inclination, which Esau embodies, has played in spurring his spiritual growth. He travels with his family to the land of his birth and sends ahead a handsome gift of atonement— hundreds of goats, sheep, camels, cows, and donkeys. While he awaits the confrontation with Esau, darkness falls. As during the incident on Mount Moriah, he is again alone.

Darkness is an important factor. During daytime hours, we tend to put on our public masks. We are dressed and groomed, polite and smiling. It is only in the dark, when our public identity is no longer visible, that fundamental and essential questions and struggles emerge: What is the meaning of life? Where am I going? Why is this happening to me? Why now? These are the same questions that confront Jacob during the lonely night before he reunites with Esau.

In the darkness, a mysterious event occurs. A stranger enters Jacob's tent and begins to wrestle with him. The Bible calls this individual an *ish*. An *ish* could be a man. An *ish* could be an angel or a divine messenger. An *ish* could be God. We can't be sure.

But Jacob clearly believes that he is struggling with God Himself, because the next day he names the place "Peniel," meaning "God's face," and proclaims, *"I have seen God face to face."*

Jacob has now encountered God in two forms. In the dream of the ladder, he saw God as his gentle protector, always with him. But this time Jacob sees God as an *ish* who initiates struggles. And the perennial nighttime questions disappear. He doesn't need to ask anymore: Why me? Why now? Now he knows God is present in both the beauty *and* the struggles of life.

The *ish* and Jacob wrestle all night long. And the struggle is evenly matched. The Bible tells us that when the *ish "saw that he had not prevailed against Jacob, he wrenched Jacob's hip at its socket."* Yet Jacob, though he must be in terrible pain, still clings to the *ish. "I will not let you go unless you bless me,"* he states.

The blessing is granted. In blessing him, the *ish* gives Jacob a new name—"Israel"—and says that the name signifies that *"you have struggled with God and people, and you have prevailed."*

The new identity means that Jacob has prevailed in his struggles with both good and evil. He has completed his journey of transformation. He need no longer constantly feel guilty while trying to wash the blood of deception from his hands. He now has the courage to confront and reconcile with his brother. He can stand erect, proud of who he is, a man guided by a mysterious, divine force, one who is worthy of becoming the leader of a nation. His battle has left a visible imprint, though. His injured thigh—to be specific, the sciatic nerve—leaves him with a limp.

All struggles leave their mark. This is also true of our life today. Every risk taken, whether physical or emotional, may cause an injury and often does. But as the Native American saying goes, "A warrior who dies without scars has fought no battles." So a person who dies without struggles has not lived.

Jacob's struggles are not completely over, however. They will continue through his children, especially through his favorite, Joseph.

7

The Favorite Son

YOU MIGHT HAVE NOTICED BY NOW THAT BIBLICAL MOTHers and fathers often had parenting problems. Take Abraham. What do you think happened to his relationship with his beloved son, Isaac, after that fateful three-day journey that ended at the top of Mount Moriah? Can a son forget being tied up on a pile of firewood while his father hovers over him with a sharp knife in his hand? Although ultimately an angel intervened, it is likely that Isaac never went for a walk with Abraham again.

Take Isaac. He had twin boys, but he favored one, Esau, while his wife, Rebecca, favored the other, Jacob. There must have been more than a few disputes in the marital tent concerning this parental difference of opinion. Esau didn't help things by his conduct, bringing home a daughter-in-law who was, as the Bible tells us, *"a source of bitterness to Isaac and Rebecca."* After the deception over the paternal blessing, the family unit was ripped apart. Esau harbored a murderous rage against his brother, and Jacob was forced to flee.

As we all know, family patterns tend to repeat themselves, so it is no surprise that Jacob, when he starts a family, is a less-than-perfect parent himself.

Jacob yearns to have a child with his beloved Rachel, but as Rachel is barren, he ends up fathering ten sons by Rachel's sister, Leah, and the maidservants Bilhah and Zilpah, who are also his wives. (At the time, polygamy, including marrying sisters, was an acceptable practice.)

Finally, after many years, Rachel does give birth to a son, Joseph, and Jacob, not surprisingly, commits a number of grave parenting errors. To begin with, the Bible tells us that Jacob *"loved Joseph best of all his sons, for he was the child of his old age."* Rachel also gives birth to a second son, Benjamin, but she dies during the course of that delivery, and Jacob grieves the loss until the end of his life.

So what does Jacob do to further distinguish Joseph from his eleven brothers? He gives him *"a coat of many colors."*

In referring to this special coat that Jacob gave Joseph, the Bible uses a strange word: *passim*. This has been translated in many different ways—as an ornamented tunic, a coat with long sleeves, a coat of colorful pieces. But the most interesting translation I've come across says it was a "dream coat."

It seems that in certain Middle Eastern cultures, this type of coat was given to members of a club that specialized in analyzing and interpreting dreams. So when Jacob sees that Joseph is a dreamer, he gives him the kind of coat that dreamers wear.

Right after Joseph begins wearing this special coat, he has a number of dreams that eventually prove to be prophetic. In one, he dreams that he is binding sheaves in the field when, suddenly, *his* sheaf stands up and the sheaves of his brothers bow to it. In another, eleven stars—one for each of his brothers—are bowing to him.

All along, Joseph's brothers have had quite a hard time dealing with their father's favoritism, and then Jacob rubs it in even more by giving Joseph this beautiful coat that you'd have to be blind to miss. To make matters even worse, Joseph compounds the problem by wearing it all the time, flaunting it. The final insult comes when Joseph begins telling everyone about the dreams he is having, saying quite plainly that someday his brothers will be subservient to him. Is it any wonder that the brothers cannot contain their hatred of Joseph any longer?

The Bible is teaching us a very important lesson here, one we have all seen played out in life many times. I call it the law of gravity. Heavy objects are not the only things that fall to the ground. People with an inflated sense of self-importance fall to the ground as well.

Joseph, as good a man as he is, suffers from an inflated ego. He's special, he knows he's special, and he acts like it. He doesn't restrain the specialness and uniqueness of who he is. So he himself is partly responsible for fueling his brothers' hatred.

Today, this happens all the time. One person's specialness, good fortune, or wealth often engenders both conscious and unconscious hostility. We've all seen someone we know "make it." The next thing you know, he's building a mansion, driving a Jaguar, and inviting all his less fortunate friends over so he can show off his new toys.

Knowing human nature, I can tell you that his friends do not cheer his success. Human nature wants balance, and sooner or later—most likely sooner—something will bring this individual to earth, because he has engendered so much conscious or unconscious hostility.

Joseph's brothers sold him into slavery. In the modern world we don't do that, but we do something else to someone who wears the coat of good fortune inappropriately—we sue. Litigation is often used to deflate an overinflated ego in an effort to bring about equality.

I am reminded of the case of Michael Milken, the Wall Street wizard who went to prison and was forced to pay millions of dollars in fines. I am not suggesting that Milken should not have been punished for his crimes, but it is possible that the impetus for investigating his ventures had a great deal to do with the fact that he was the wealthiest entrepreneur on Wall Street. He was making what was described by prosecutors as "obscene" amounts of money, and a great many people were anxious to cut him down to size. Others were certain that such vast wealth could not have been acquired honestly. (As it turned out, part of it hadn't been.)

Often, when a movie is a huge hit, several people file suit claiming that they originated the idea. As one famous filmmaker who has fought off a number of such suits put it, "People don't sue over flops."

Litigation in families is also quite common. One particularly vicious Yiddish curse, cited by the late film director Ernst Lubitsch, goes like this: "You should have a lot of money, but you should be the only one in your family with it." One can just imagine what might happen to that fortunate—or should we say unfortunate?—family member.

We learn from the story of Joseph that it is good to be a dreamer and it is good to be loved, but you can't parade your blessings in a way that makes other people who are not blessed in the same way feel diminished.

The same goes for Jacob. It's good to love your children and to appreciate the qualities that distinguish them from one another, but you can't make one such an obvious favorite that the others feel cheated. Yet this is a common occurrence in our society. It's such a common lament: "Mom always liked you best." Unfortunately, the consequences are quite profound, haunting children into and through adulthood.

I know of one such family in which the parents treated their two children, a boy and a girl, quite differently. The girl was the golden child, blond and fair, in addition to her other endearing traits. The boy, who was olive-skinned and dark-haired, was considered the black sheep of the family. It didn't help matters when the girl was killed in a car accident. She then took on mythical qualities of goodness and perfection, and he, the survivor, became a nonentity who could never measure up to his parents' expectations.

The son tried hard to win his parents' approval. Although he never became the doctor his parents wanted him to be, he did form his own very successful company, got married, had a child, and lived a good life. But his parents' attitude had left scars. He spent years in therapy, trying to sort out his feelings of inferiority.

His parents hurt themselves by their behavior, too. After the father died, the mother was left alone, mourning her husband, mourning her daughter, and estranged from her son, who all his life had only wanted her approval; she became a lonely, bitter old woman.

How can a son honor and respect a mother who acts like this? Such behavior by parents clearly causes a lack of self-esteem in their children, but it also creates problems for those trying to obey the commandment to honor one's parents.

At this juncture, I might point out that the commandment "Honor your father and your mother" does not include honoring the unhealthy part of your parents. Contrary to common misunderstanding, you are not obliged to honor your parents' alcoholism, their miserliness, their self-pity or bitterness, or any other destructive behavior. However, you are duty bound to find good things about your parents to respect. There is good in every person, and this is what you are meant to honor.

Nevertheless, when parents behave badly, it is hard for a child to see the good behind the toxicity. In such a situation a child is forced to make a choice between living with feelings of bitterness toward his or her parents and forgiving them.

It is no coincidence that the Bible's chief model of forgiveness is none other than Joseph, as we will see next.

8

Fate Versus Destiny

Y OU MAY RECALL THAT IN JOSEPH'S STORY, HIS BROTHERS throw him into a pit filled with snakes and scorpions, intending for him to die there. But then the brothers have a change of heart, realizing they can get rid of Joseph and make some money in the process. So they sell him into slavery instead.

This is an awful thing to do to Joseph, the favorite son, who has been coddled by his adoring father. Thrust into a cruel foreign environment, he could easily be broken by the experience, both emotionally and physically. He could become bitter and angry, toiling away at his slave labor and feeling sorry for himself.

But that is not how he deals with his fate. It is interesting to study the transformation that takes place in his character from the self-centered youth who gloated about his dreams and his unique gifts to a fine, upstanding young man of tremendous moral strength.

We see the first sign of this change when Joseph chooses not to curse his fate. Indeed, he makes the most of the situation and is rewarded for his efforts. The Bible tells us, *"The Lord was with Joseph, and he was a successful man."*

Joseph's new self is certainly put to the test more than once. Just when he has earned the esteem of his Egyptian master and has been placed in charge of the household, his master's wife tries to seduce him, for, we are told, *"Joseph was well built and handsome."* But Joseph passes this test admirably. He refuses to betray the trust his master has placed in him and resists the wife's seduction. Finally, after her numerous advances are rebuffed, the scorned woman falsely accuses Joseph of trying to rape her, and he is unjustly thrown into jail.

This is another instance when a weaker man might bemoan his fate, lose his faith in God, or give up on life, but Joseph once again turns adversity into opportunity, fate into destiny.

Joseph's concern for his fellow inmates creates an opportunity for him to demonstrate his talent for interpreting dreams. Eventually, this gift brings him to the attention of the pharaoh, a man troubled by nightmares, and Joseph rises to a position of great power. Then the final test comes. Joseph is given the chance to get even with his brothers when they come to Egypt to beg for food in a time of famine. Instead, he welcomes them with open arms, weeping with joy. The scene describing their reunion is among the most moving in the Bible.

The brothers, who do not recognize Joseph in his Egyptian finery and, for that matter, cannot fathom that life could have turned the tables on them in this way, are dumbfounded.

But Joseph urges them forward. *"Come near to me. . . . I am Joseph, your brother, he whom you sold into Egypt."*

One can imagine why they are speechless. The brother they tried to kill now has an opportunity to take revenge, and he can take it in many ways. He can order them slain on the spot, have them thrown into jail, or simply deny them the food they seek, thereby sentencing them to slow death by starvation.

But Joseph does none of these things. He is so happy to see his brothers that he does not even demand that they beg his forgiveness. He tells them that they have no need to apologize. And here he makes one of the most dramatic statements in the entire Bible: *"Now, do not be distressed or reproach yourself because you sold me into Egypt. God sent me ahead of you to save life on the earth . . . and to ensure your survival. . . . So it was not you who sent me here, but God."*

Joseph understands that all the misfortunes that have befallen him have had a higher purpose: They have set forth a chain of events that has allowed him to be placed in a position of power in which he is able to save not only his brothers but the entire nation of Israel.

This is what I mean when I say that Joseph turned his fate into his destiny. Had he wasted his energy hating his brothers and feeling sorry for himself, he would have been too demoralized to be of service to others and to distinguish himself. His fate would have remained his fate.

Unfortunately, a great many people allow their fate to remain their fate. In fact, they choose to focus on the evil that has befallen them, never searching for meaning, direction, or opportunity in the experience.

For example, I know one young man whose father was largely absent during his formative years. A successful filmmaker whose work took him away on location much of the time, the father put his career ahead of his family, and his son knew it. Now in his thirties, the son still harbors a great deal of resentment toward his father. The son's long-festering bitterness not only makes it impossible to build a relationship with his father, who is now retired, it also infects his relationships with other members of his family, as well as with his friends and coworkers. In blaming everything that goes wrong on his father, the son is ruining his own life.

Contrast the above example to that of another young man I know. His father abandoned the family completely when he was a child, and he was raised by his mother under difficult circumstances. This man could rightly question the fate that caused him to be raised without the emotional or financial security of a father. Instead, he devotes his spare time to an organization that counsels troubled teenagers from single-parent families. Raised without a father, he has turned his fate into his destiny, becoming a father to many fatherless boys.

The most inspiring example I know of a person accepting his fate and turning it, by sheer force of will, into his destiny is that of Jim MacLaren, a young man who is the closest contemporary parallel to Joseph I have ever known.

Like Joseph, Jim began his young adult life with the world in his pocket. He was handsome, talented, intelligent, and athletic. A student at Yale, he was the quarterback for the university's football team; he excelled in his studies and was beginning a promising career in acting. But it was not to be. While riding his motorcycle in Manhattan, Jim was struck by a bus that ran a red light. He survived several weeks in a coma, regaining consciousness only to learn that his left leg had been amputated.

But Jim accepted his fate. In fact, he became obsessed with proving that a one-legged man could accomplish athletic feats few whole-bodied men could. He trained vigorously to compete in triathlons, which required him to run, bicycle, and swim great distances. His achievements led to a contract with a major sportswear company, and he was a favorite on the inspirational lecture circuit.

But then fate served up another test for Jim. While bicycling in a triathlon near Los Angeles, he was hit by a van that had circumvented a police barricade. He ended up in a hospital, this time as a quadriplegic.

Perhaps the most remarkable thing about this dramatic story— a truth more incredible than fiction—was Jim's attitude toward this horrible fate. Jim's first words when he learned he was totally paralyzed were "I wonder what I'm supposed to learn from this." Like Joseph, Jim immediately perceived that there could be a higher purpose to what had happened to him.

Jim is now well on his way to forging his destiny. After he accepted that he would remain a quadriplegic and entered a rehabilitation center to learn how best to deal with his handicap, doctors discovered and removed a blood clot in his neck that had been interfering with nerve impulses. Jim has now regained his ability to walk, although he can do so only with the aid of crutches. But he's not wasting any time; he is back to work on the lecture circuit, moving audiences to tears with his story. He is living proof that Bible stories are not tales of imaginary beings so noble that their actions cannot be duplicated in our time. Jim is flesh and blood, a real person, who did not curse his fate. Like Joseph, he has found in every "wrong" turn an opportunity to blaze a new path.

There is another aspect to the Joseph story that we have not yet examined: Joseph's astonishing ability to forgive his brothers.

It is hard to pinpoint exactly when he forgives them. In the Bible, the words "I forgive" are never recorded. By the time Joseph confronts his brothers, forgiveness is not even an issue; he simply tells them that they need have no regrets. Only later does he mention in passing that what they did was wrong.

Joseph's forgiving attitude is hard to achieve, especially when you have been terribly wronged by another person. In the case of Joseph, his life could have been ruined by the actions of his brothers. However, it was not, because he did not allow that to happen.

I firmly believe, based on the experiences of the many people I treat in therapy, that a great many human problems are self-inflicted. True, the emotional injury often begins with a wrong done by someone else. But the hurt and anger and inability to forgive fester like a wound that eventually grows gangrenous and threatens one's life.

The medical analogy is not farfetched, since many people actually are physically affected by their emotions. How many heart attacks are the result of "psychic cholesterol" clogging the coronary arteries? We must forgive those who have wronged us. If we cannot forgive them with an open heart, we should forgive them anyway, simply because it is bad *for us* if we don't.

M. Scott Peck offers excellent advice on this very issue in his *Further Along the Road Less Traveled.* He writes:

> The process of forgiveness—indeed, the chief reason for forgiveness—is selfish. The reason to forgive others is not for their sake. They are not likely to know that they need to be forgiven. They're not likely to remember their offense. They are likely to say, "You made it up." They may even be dead. The reason to forgive is for our own sake. For our own health. Because beyond that point needed for healing, if we hold on to our anger, we stop growing and our souls begin to shrivel.

To that excellent advice, I add one bit of my own: If you cannot forgive, act as if you can. Pretend that you have forgiven the people who have wronged you, and extend your hand to them. Call to wish them happy birthday. Inquire about their health.

Pretend that you have the ability to forgive as Joseph did. Alcoholics Anonymous says, "Fake it to make it." I say, pretend to be a little like the religious models of the Bible. A little pious pretentiousness never hurt anybody. You might surprise yourself—before you realize it, you might not even be pretending.

But if you do not even try, one thing is certain. Nursing your hurt feelings, your anger, and your bitterness will not bring you happiness. It will only make you a slave to your fate, and you may never come to know that you could have freed yourself—that you could have been the master of your destiny.

9

Angels

THUS FAR, WE HAVE LOOKED AT THREE VERY INTERESTING men, Abraham, Jacob, and Joseph, each one of whom was quite human and flawed. But these men became immortalized in the pages of the Bible as models for the rest of humanity because they struggled with their shortcomings and accomplished great things that changed history forever.

The secret is that they didn't do it alone. They had special helpers. And the good news is that these helpers are still in business. Their services are available twenty-four hours a day—just dial 1-800-ANGEL.

Forgive the little joke. But I'm not kidding about angels and their ability to help us anywhere, anytime.

Angels are divine messengers that God sends to us in crucial moments. Their presence endows us with the strength to make valiant efforts in moments of fear or simply serves as a reassurance in our moments of loneliness. Often angels watch over us in times of danger, conveying warnings. But they can also share our joy or communicate good news.

When these messengers appear in the Bible, they are sometimes identified as angels but are often described as mysterious strangers who bring important messages. They appear at key moments, and their interventions change history.

For example, three mysterious strangers come to visit Abraham, who is ninety-nine years old and just recovering from his circumcision. Their purpose, among others, is to tell Abraham that he and his similarly aged wife, Sarah, will have a child. It is astonishing news indeed, since Sarah has been barren all her life and is well past menopause.

Shortly thereafter, in answer to Abraham's prayer, angels rescue his nephew Lot and Lot's family from Sodom and Gomorrah before the two cities are destroyed.

Later, an angel stays Abraham's hand as he is about to sacrifice his beloved son, Isaac.

Joseph has an encounter with a mysterious stranger while searching for his brothers in the pastures. As in the passage in which Jacob is struggling with a mysterious being, the Bible uses the word *ish* to describe the man who directs Joseph and then disappears.

The Bible is telling us that we, too, can expect to meet an *ish* an angel. This person may be totally unknown to us, and we may never meet this person again, but we will know that the encounter was really special, conveying a divine message to guide us.

In the case of Joseph, the *ish* directs him to his brothers, who are plotting his death. What initially transpires between Joseph and his brothers seems disastrous, but in the end it serves to transform Joseph's life and eventually to save his family and descendants from certain starvation.

A colleague of mine, a fellow psychotherapist, had a similar experience while applying for admission to the University of Southern California's clinical psychology department. He knew that only five out of some eight hundred applicants were accepted each year, and he waited for the results with sweaty palms. Then he got a call from a mysterious stranger, who offered to duplicate his application and submit it to the counseling psychology department. As it happened, he did not gain admission into clinical psychology, but he did go on to become an outstanding student in counseling psychology and a highly respected psychotherapist. Today, he says, "I find it fascinating that a person I've never even met was the most instrumental in shaping my career."

Most of us have experienced at least one such situation in our lives. Someone helps us in a way that may or may not be immediately significant. But when we want to thank that *ish,* we turn around and he is gone. We should direct our thanks to God, because it is He who sends us the *ish.*

In the Five Books of Moses, the angels are never named; they are mysterious beings. Later, in the Book of Daniel, two archangels are identified by name: Gabriel, the angel of strength, and Michael, the guardian angel. Tradition also names, among others, Raphael, the angel of healing, and Uriel, the angel of light. Tradition has it that it was Michael who stilled Abraham's hand as he was about to sacrifice Isaac and that Raphael was one of the three strangers who visited Abraham following his circumcision, to aid in his healing.

I have a friend who is convinced that she had an encounter with an angel in a moment of great distress. She was at an airport seeing a friend off when his helicopter collided with a small plane. The plane exploded in midair, while the helicopter crashed to the ground. She ran through the debris to help her friend get out of the wreckage, not hearing people scream at her, "Get away, it's gonna blow!" But as she scrambled helplessly, trying to reach her friend in the wreckage, with the engine still running and fuel leaking everywhere, the warnings penetrated: "Get away, it's gonna blow!" She was momentarily confused—should she help her friend or save herself?

Then, as she tells the story, a man appeared. He had a mass of strawberry blond curls and was wearing a dirty white T-shirt. He was holding a tiny fire extinguisher. His presence gave her the strength she needed. She was sure that, if a fire started, he'd put it out. She returned to aid her friend.

"I *knew* it was the archangel Gabriel," she recalls today. "I don't know why I gave him that name, why not another angel. I had no idea that Gabriel was considered the angel of strength. But this man"—who subsequently disappeared and could not be identified by any of the other witnesses at the scene—"gave me the strength I needed at that moment. I knew that, with him there, everything would be all right." And it was. The wreckage did not blow up, and her friend not only survived the crash but recovered from his injuries.

The wonderful thing about angels is that they can be called upon for help whenever we need it. Indeed, an old Hebrew prayer instructs us to do just that. The prayer, meant to be recited before going to sleep, recalls the experience of Jacob. He went to sleep on Mount Moriah feeling totally dejected and utterly alone, but he dreamt of a ladder reaching to heaven, with angels ascending and descending, surrounded by God's presence. As a result of that dream, Jacob realized that he had divine assistance with him at all times. So do we. Before we go to sleep and dream, a special prayer connects us with Jacob's experience: "May Michael be at my right hand, Gabriel at my left, Uriel before me, Raphael behind me, and above my head the presence of God."

I have thought of that prayer on many occasions when I have had to perform a difficult task. I will never forget one time when I was to perform the marriage ceremony of a prominent couple. I had officiated at many wedding ceremonies, but never in the presence of an audience packed with so many distinguished people. They were all expecting me to say something profound, and I knew their standards of performance were very high.

I called on the angels and imagined them standing there, one on my left and another on my right. Suddenly, my nervousness disappeared and my speech flowed. I am certain that no one in attendance suspected how intimidating the task had seemed to me just moments before.

With angels around, you need never feel scared or alone. You can feel strong, empowered. It is no accident that the Hebrew word for "angel," *malach,* is similar to the word for "king," *melech.* When angels empower you, you possess the courage and strength of a king.

There is another lesson here for all of us: We can become angels for other people. When we empower others to feel better about themselves, when we inspire them to do good, when we reassure them and help them feel less alone, we serve as angels.

I find the hospital where I work to be full of angels—or at least of people who do a good job of imitating angels. More than one patient whom I have sought to comfort has become a source of comfort and enlightenment to me.

And I am convinced that angels sometimes pop up entirely by surprise in guises that are meant to confound us. I am constantly astonished to find inspiring messages coming from people whom I would least expect to be messengers of God.

Some years back, one such person came into my Bible class. The study group was made up largely of doctors, nurses, and other health care professionals, all well dressed in crisply pressed uniforms or lab coats. But one woman came in wearing tattered, disheveled clothes. She looked like one of the homeless people we see all too frequently on our city streets—and as it turned out, she was.

Some of the people in the class were disturbed by her presence. When she showed up again, several came to me to suggest that something needed to be done to discourage her from returning. I decided not to intervene.

As it turned out, this woman was brilliant. I still don't know why she had become homeless, but she was a tremendous asset to the class. Her contributions were often original and penetrating. I am convinced she was an angel.

I still think about her often. I am happy to say that her insights have stayed with me and that they have found their way here— into the pages of this book.

10

The Art of Dying

IF YOU ARE ABOUT TO HAVE A BABY, YOU CAN GO TO THE bookstore and find more books on the process of birthing than you can carry home. The same is true if you are about to get married. Dozens of volumes will provide you with advice on selecting your wedding dress, tuxedo, and caterer. Dozens more will help you plan every detail of your honeymoon.

There are also books on death and dying. But oddly enough, they do not address the spiritual nature of the dying process. Yet isn't dying as significant as other life-cycle events?

I would suggest that dying is perhaps even more significant— and certainly more frightening—than all the other rites of passage we experience. But there are no manuals out there. Fortunately, the Bible can be a manual of a sort.

First, and most important, the Bible is a manual for living that, if followed, should make dying a great deal less mysterious and less frightening.

Second, through the examples of the deaths of the patriarchs, the Bible offers us inspiration about how we should behave as the end of life approaches.

In this chapter, we examine the death of Jacob and see what lessons it might hold for us today.

As the story begins, Joseph is at his dying father's bedside. Joseph was the son who had received special gifts from God, who had risen to the challenges and tests of life, who had repeatedly demonstrated his integrity in the most difficult situations, and who, through his power to forgive, was the most loving and giving of all of Jacob's sons.

Would that we were all so fortunate to have a Joseph with us at the time of our death—someone completely trustworthy to carry out our dying wishes, someone kind and loving to see us through those last moments when we feel most vulnerable.

I learned just how essential this support is from a patient who, shortly before his death, called me to his bedside with numerous theological questions. I tried to answer them as well as I could, but I realized I could not, even with my best intellectual arguments, resolve his questions of faith and doubts about God. At a loss, I simply held his hand, prayed with him, and assured him that I'd be back. Something told me to continue my visits with him, and I did, more frequently than I ordinarily would have. As I went back time after time to hold his hand and be with him for a little while, his questions and doubts seemed to disappear. I realized that he merely wanted a little bit of caring, a little bit of love.

When love is present, so is God, and the intellectual doubts melt away.

I TELL MY PATIENTS THAT DYING IS NOT MUCH DIFFERENT A RITE OF passage than being born. Indeed, the Nobel Prize–winning author Hermann Hesse observes in *Narcissus and Goldmund* that in birth, death, and sex, the moans, groans, and facial expressions are very much alike. But if death is a kind of birth, the person who is with us at that moment serves as a kind of midwife. We want this person to be gentle, loving, and nurturing.

Who would you want to be with you at that important time? One of my patients told me, "I certainly don't want my wife to be there—she'll just tell me I'm doing it the wrong way."

It's a funny remark but also a sad one. Because a death, while obviously stressful for relatives, who are experiencing a tremendous sense of loss, often brings out the worst in people.

I have officiated at many a funeral for which seating arrangements proved to be extremely difficult because so many relatives were not speaking to one another. At one such funeral, the widow and a son from a previous marriage were clearly bitter enemies, and they subsequently ended up suing each other over the inheritance. A year later, when the widow asked me to unveil the tombstone that was being erected, I asked if her stepson would be invited to the ceremony.

"Absolutely not. I never want to see him again," she told me flatly.

"But this was his father. Wouldn't he want to be present?" I pressed.

"I don't care what he wants. I paid for the tombstone," she retorted.

I didn't tell her that although she might own the tombstone, she didn't own her husband's body. I did tell her that under the circumstances I couldn't be present. That was the last I heard from her. I wish that at the funeral she and her stepson had been able to bury their hurt and anger while burying their husband and father.

Many people who anticipate such problems try to prevent family squabbles by writing wills that set forth not only their wishes as to the distribution of their assets but also their wishes as to the behavior of their heirs.

This is an excellent idea. Jack Riemer has written several good books on ethical wills that explain how such a document might be written. But I also believe that the best advice a parent can give his or her own children on living an ethical life is to have lived one. A picture, after all, is worth a thousand words.

I have frequently suggested to my clients—those who are healthy and have every reason to expect a long life ahead—that they should imagine themselves at their own funeral, listening to the eulogy. What are they likely to hear others saying about them? Is it what they would want to hear? If not, it's time for a change— time to begin living the kind of life that will result in a eulogy they'd be proud to hear and an obituary they'd be proud to read.

Alfred B. Nobel, the inventor of dynamite, had the opportunity to read his own obituary when on the occasion of his brother's death, a newspaper printed his death notice by mistake. Nobel was dismayed to see himself described as the inventor of methods of destruction, and he took great pains to make sure that he would be remembered otherwise. He endowed his vast wealth to those who do good in the world, and today his Nobel Prizes are the first things that come to mind when we hear his name.

So imagine a similar mistake has been made in the newspaper regarding yourself. Read the obituary—there is still time to edit it.

Of course, these days many people are preoccupied with how they might die. Some of the "living wills" that are being written are quite altruistic; their authors are concerned that their organs be donated so that others might live or that their assets go to their loved ones and not be wasted on expensive technology that might keep them endlessly alive in a vegetative state. But there is also a less altruistic motive in some of the "do not resuscitate" directives—once the dying process has begun, people don't want to be made to suffer while machines force them to live. This is also the motive behind the so-called right-to-die movement.

In direct opposition, another movement has arisen—the conscious dying movement. Those who want to be conscious while dying don't mind bearing the pain. Frequently, they feel that the pain is an essential part of the process that makes them ready for what is to come. In other cases, they simply do not want their senses dulled by morphine—they want to be aware of every part of their transition.

If you think of dying as a kind of birthing, being made unconscious would be like sleeping through your birthday celebration.

I was privileged to be present at one such death recently. Sometime before, the patient, "Steven," and I discussed the passage in the Bible in which God creates Adam and blows the breath of life into his nostrils. We talked about the kabbalistic notion that each breath we inhale is not a breath we "take" but one that is "given" to us by God. We also spoke of dying as God's last kiss, the moment when the breath of life is retrieved.

Steven's death was not easy, and sometime before it, he lost the ability to speak. His family and I were gathered around him, offering as much love and support as we could. Moments before his death, Steven looked up at us and brought his fingers to his lips as if to blow us a kiss. With tears in our eyes, we understood what he was telling us: He had felt the kiss of God. And then he was gone.

Another example of this type of conscious death is related by Kirk Douglas in his autobiography, *The Ragman's Son.* Douglas's mother, Bryna—by all accounts a kind and God-loving woman— died a most peaceful death. She reminded her son to light candles for the Sabbath, and then she looked up at him lovingly and smiled. "Don't be scared. . . . It happens to all of us," she reassured him. Holding his breath, he watched her breathe slowly until she let out a long breath and did not inhale again. On her face was an expression he described as "clear and serene." She entered the beyond unafraid, ready for what awaited her.

Bryna's and Steven's loving messages to us echo the message we find in the Bible regarding the death of Jacob. Jacob hugs and kisses Joseph's two sons—his grandchildren—clearly treating the younger with greater deference than the older, the firstborn. Having suffered much as a result of an accident of birth, he now leaves his "ethical will"—in effect saying to Joseph, "Treat all your children as if they were your firstborn; the spiritual legacy is open to everyone."

Then he gathers all his sons around him and blesses each one, prophesying their futures and those of their descendants. Then, the Bible tells us, *"When Jacob finished his instructions to his sons, he drew his feet into the bed and, breathing his last, he was gathered to his people."*

Note that, on dying, Jacob assumes the fetal position—he is ready for the "birthing" that is about to take place. Note also that, in dying, he is not alone; he understands that he is returning to his father, Isaac, his mother, Rebecca, his grandfather Abraham, and his grandmother Sarah.

The dying process need not be lonely for us. We leave our living family behind, only to join the family that has gone before us.

One of my clients, a man of seventy-eight who is quite robust and healthy in every respect, tells me he often thinks of his mother and father. Something tells me that he is getting ready to join them—just as they are getting ready for him—although I am not sure that his own children are ready to let him go.

All of Jacob's sons were ready, but the loss of their father nevertheless filled them with grief. When Jacob died, the Bible tells us, *"Joseph flung himself upon his father's face and wept over him and kissed him."*

Joseph's kiss was not wasted on a cold body. It was a loving touch that reached into the beyond, because Joseph recognized that his father was alive in another realm. But while Joseph was a highly spiritual person who knew this, he was also very human—he had lost his father, and he was brokenhearted.

When you lose someone you love, allow yourself to grieve. Close the doors and cry your heart out. Mourn with others. You need the time off, no matter how spiritually elevated you might be.

Death is as stressful as birth. The new baby comes home, and much has changed. The family dynamic must be rearranged, and it is appropriate to take maternity or paternity leave. So it is with death. Take the time, do it right. And remember, it happens to all of us.

PART II

11

The Birth of a Hero

As we end the first of the Five Books of Moses, the Book of Genesis, we are left with two very graphic images of another kind of end, death—the death of Jacob and the death of his son Joseph. It is fitting that the second of the Five Books of Moses, the Book of Exodus, should begin with a birth, the birth of a child who will be named Moses.

Like fast cuts in a film, these images are stunning in their similarity: Joseph being placed in a casket; the infant Moses being placed in a different type of casket, a basket, that his mother will float down the Nile to save his life.

The Bible tells us that the descendants of Jacob, now known by the patriarch's name as Israelites, have been living and prospering in Egypt ever since Joseph saved them from the famine. But the debt the pharaoh owed Joseph has now been forgotten, and the new pharaoh fears that the Israelites have become too numerous and too well entrenched in Egypt.

This is a common reaction, one we have seen repeated on numerous occasions. When a foreign or minority group within a country expands, the natives grow hostile. Then begin deportations and restrictions such as those we've seen in Europe, particularly Germany, in recent years. Even in America, we are seeing aggressive campaigns being waged against immigrants and increasing animosity toward all minorities by those who fear the loss of their dominance.

Such was the climate in Egypt. The motivation that caused the pharaoh to enslave and oppress the Israelites was as old as time—insecurity. He feared a challenge to his power base, and he reacted with venom.

We see this kind of behavior repeated today. When people are insecure, either consciously or unconsciously, they want to be pharaoh. They want to dominate others, control them, and imprison them within psychological boundaries. Husbands do it to wives, wives to husbands, parents to children, employers to employees, teachers to students, and friends to friends.

It is interesting that it is often the most powerful who are the most insecure. Who would ever think the mighty pharaoh would feel threatened? But he is. He is so stricken with fear that when his ruthlessness, cruelty, and harsh labor practices fail to bring about the desired results, he devises a horrifying method of keeping the Israelites down: He orders that all newborn male children be thrown into the Nile.

It must have been a terrible time to be alive. How could a husband and wife, in the midst of such oppression and horror, still have enough hope to have children? How could they make love, knowing that if a male child was conceived, he would be doomed to certain death and they to unspeakable grief? Yet the urge to procreate is one of the strongest human drives. In the most devastating of circumstances—during famines and wars, even the Holocaust—children have been born.

So this male child, destined to be the most famous and most heroic figure in the Bible, is born under extremely adverse conditions. Indeed, a hero could not arrive in this world any other way.

Every civilization has its heroes, real or mythological, and each arrives in this world under adverse conditions, or at least with difficulty. I often tell mothers who have given birth to premature babies and are agonizing over their well-being that such a child might be a hero in the making. Parents can sense this for themselves when they visit the neonatal unit in the hospital where I am chaplain. At first, they see only the pint-sized babies, who are wired, bandaged, and intubated, struggling for life in their incubators. But eventually, they begin to notice the photos that are prominently displayed on the walls—pictures of former patients, now happy, healthy, smiling children, who provide silent testimony to the promising future that can await even the most fragile infant. I am certain that, whether or not these neonates end up as heroes to the world, to their parents they will always serve as reminders of a heroic battle for survival.

I also emphasize to new mothers who pray for an easy life for their babies that challenges may help to form character.

One of my clients—a young woman who suffered both sexual and emotional abuse as a child and who overcame those traumatic experiences—told me she now faces a disturbing dilemma. As a new mother, she knows she will do anything in her power to ensure that her child never experiences such traumas; she is prepared to protect her little girl with her own life if need be. Yet she realizes that her own best qualities were forged from the horrors of her childhood and that her child will have to encounter some pain in order to grow.

"How can I protect my child from pain and yet be certain that she will grow up to be a great person?" she asks. Thus far, she has come up with no answers, but she has resolved to teach her child well, so that when adversity arrives—as it surely will—her daugh-

ter will be ready for the challenge and will learn from the experience.

MOSES SURVIVES HIS BIRTH ONLY TO BE PLUNGED INTO FURTHER AD-
versity. And his own mother is responsible for the symbolic expression of that. While other baby boys are being thrown into the Nile,
she chooses that very river as the means of his salvation. She makes
a waterproof basket and sends him off to meet his fate. The basket
is floating down the Nile when it attracts the attention of the
pharaoh's daughter, who delivers him to her father's court. So twice
the infant Moses is sent into the jaws of death: first into the waters
of the Nile, then into the hands of the very pharaoh who would
seek his doom.

Water has important connotations for the heroes of humanity.
It is the basic element that sustains life. In addition, a fetus is nurtured in water (the amniotic fluid), so it has come to symbolize re-
birth. Indeed, rituals in various cultures and religions, such as the
conversion ceremony in Judaism and baptism in certain denomi-
nations of Christianity, acknowledge this by requiring immersion
in water.

Another aspect common to heroes is that they are often raised
by more than one mother. Moses has both humble and royal beginnings, and in the tension of these opposites he develops the diverse characteristics he will need as a leader.

It is unfortunate that in our American society the extended family, with grandparents fulfilling the role of surrogate parents, has
diminished. Many of my clients who were raised in other cultures
speak fondly of the influence their "second set of parents" had
upon them.

A woman I know was raised by her two grandmothers after her
mother had a nervous breakdown. One grandmother was a quiet,
religious woman who read to her constantly and inspired her to
pursue a career as a writer. The other grandmother was illiterate

and secular, with a passionate nature. She showered her granddaughter with affection and taught her the meaning of love.

Moses's upbringing is similarly affected by diverse influences. The influence of his humble mother causes him to identify with the oppressed and to strike out against injustice. His royal upbringing teaches him about power and gives him the self-confidence he needs to assume leadership later.

We are told very little about Moses's life in the pharaoh's court. But what little we do know is significant and dramatic. One day, upon seeing an Israelite slave being beaten by an Egyptian taskmaster, Moses kills the perpetrator and buries his body in the sand. Biblical scholars have puzzled over this passage: Why does Moses react so strongly? Is his action prompted by an emotional identification with his own oppressed people? Yet it seems his people do not identify with him. Indeed, it is an Israelite who informs against Moses to the pharaoh. Rejected by all, with a price on his head, Moses has no choice but to flee.

Each of the great figures before him—Abraham, Jacob, and Joseph—faced a similar trial. Each had to abandon what was familiar, becoming a "stranger in a strange land" as a prelude to his own internal journey. So, too, must Moses.

Most of us should be able to identify with him in one way or another. As members of the most mobile society in the world, we change our places of residence more often, and move greater distances, than any other people on earth. Thus most of us have encountered the insecurity of finding ourselves in a strange city, having to ask directions and adapt to new customs. How much more difficult this experience must be for immigrants from a foreign country, who must learn a new language and a whole new culture when they come here. The life of a stranger—or worse, an outcast—is a lonely one, as we learn from the story of Moses.

During his flight into the desert, Moses reaches a well, there witnessing another act of injustice. Several young women want to water their flocks, but the shepherds refuse them access. Moses rises to defend the women, not knowing that they are the daughters of Jethro, a priest of Midian, who has been excommunicated for questioning the power of the local gods.

Moses joins this outcast family, marries one of its young women, and names his firstborn son Gershom, from the Hebrew word *ger,* meaning "stranger."

He settles down to a simple, solitary life tending sheep. This must have been a dramatic change of lifestyle for someone who had grown up in the comforts of the pharaoh's court.

The pharaoh's court was full of servants coming and going, of banquets and festivities. In such a setting, it would have been hard for Moses to have the total peace and quiet that fields and sheep could provide. In further contrast to the desert, the beauty of the pharaoh's court came from man-made objects rather than natural wonders. The palace's exquisite architecture, furnishings, and jewelry testified to the artistry and ingenuity of man. But in the awesome beauty of nature—the sheer majesty of mountains and the gentle roll of verdant oases—it is God's handiwork that confronts Moses at every turn. This, then, is Moses's new life, a life of solitary contemplation and inner transformation that will prepare him for the greatest challenge of his life—leading his people out of captivity.

When Moses begins this quiet life, we know he is already invested with some character traits that every leader should possess. He has enormous empathy with the downtrodden (as we saw in his reaction to the beating of a slave). He is a prudent man (he buried the Egyptian he killed). And he is not easily diverted from his commitment to justice (despite his betrayal by the very people he was trying to help, he does not hesitate to aid others in trouble, such as the young women at the well).

Yet Moses is not yet ready for the greatest mission of his life. Indeed, it will take him years to get ready, to achieve a true inner strength. We know that Moses spent a *lifetime* being a humble shepherd, since we are told that he is eighty years old when he is called upon to lead his people out of bondage.

The call comes dramatically. Unlike Abraham's quiet conversations with God or the dreams that inspired Jacob, Moses's call is a vision. The Bible tells us, *"An angel of the Lord appeared to him in a blazing fire out of a bush. He {Moses} gazed, and there was a bush all aflame, yet the bush was not consumed."* This remarkable bush that burns but is not consumed symbolizes eternity. It burns continuously, yet it is indestructible.

Within us, the spark that links us to the eternal flame also burns continuously—hope against the greatest of odds, love in the midst of hate, the will to persevere when survival seems impossible—testifying to the indestructibility of the eternal within us.

Then God Himself speaks to Moses out of the flames, saying, *"Do not come closer. Remove your shoes from your feet, for the place on which you stand is holy ground."*

What can this mean? Why must Moses take off his shoes?

Shoes are protection from the harshness of the ground, and Moses is being told that he should divest himself of anything that might be a barrier between himself and the ground upon which he walks. He is to feel the earth beneath him, the pebbles and grains of sand under the soles of his feet. This sensitivity will be necessary for him to lead; a leader's sensitivity must be fine-tuned to the feelings of his people.

Most of us are frequently surprised to discover that we have not been sensitive to the feelings of those around us. We make offhand remarks and then are astonished to find that our words have hurt. Some people are unaware of how much pain their insensitivity inflicts, often simply because they are preoccupied with their own feelings, their own insecurity.

Moses learns that if he hopes to rescue his people, he cannot be like the man he will soon oppose, the pharaoh. Moses must set aside his own feelings and become sensitive to the pain of the people who will look to him for leadership. They will be frightened, and he will have to be sensitive to their fears in order to lead effectively.

None of us is likely to be called upon to free half a million slaves, but we are bound to be called to experience a burning bush on a symbolic level. So when a friend in pain comes to you, take off your shoes and feel the sand and pebbles beneath your feet. Be sensitive to what is being confided to you.

I do not know if William Blake was thinking of the story of Moses when he wrote the poem "Auguries of Innocence," but he sums up its message perfectly:

> To see a World in a Grain of Sand,
> And a Heaven in a Wild Flower,
> Hold Infinity in the palm of your hand,
> And Eternity in an hour.

Moses will soon feel as if he is holding infinity in the palm of his hand, as his rod, by a miracle of God, changes into a serpent. He will wield that rod before the pharaoh—whose crown featured a golden spitting cobra—and he will strike at the very heart of the pharaoh's insecurity, the symbol of his power.

Then he will demand, *"Let my people go."*

12

A New Moon Rising

So THE BATTLE BEGINS: GOD VERSUS THE PHARAOH, GOOD versus evil. It must have seemed to all who witnessed the horror of the plagues—such as the Nile River, the Egyptian symbol of life, running with blood and bringing death in its wake—that their very world was being destroyed. The Israelites, intimidated by their years of servitude and oppression, were no less terrified than the Egyptians. And perhaps because of their fears, in the midst of the worst of times, God gives the Israelites a new symbol: the moon.

We have already seen that the Bible is replete with symbols, and some of the most powerful of these appear in the Book of Exodus. Here, the Bible teaches us that even when we are in the midst of tragedy, we are given something hopeful to which we can cling. There will always be a sign, a symbol to guide us. While we are in the depths of darkness, the answers will always be there. In the darkest night, we can look up and see the light of the rising moon.

Note that God's symbols, as presented in the Bible, are generally elements of nature: a tree, a rainbow, a rock. The Bible imbues these natural elements with meaning, and each symbol is intended to give us strength to face the challenges that arise.

So when the pharaoh's rage is unleashed as he is threatened with the last of the ten plagues—the death of all firstborn Egyptian males—the Israelites are told to look to the new moon.

The new moon silently speaks to them of renewal, of a new beginning. The moon returns each night to light the darkness, changing its shape, waxing and waning, only to rise afresh after a cycle of twenty-eight days. It speaks to them of the cyclical nature of life.

Just as the Israelites are getting ready to leave Egypt, they are given not only a symbol of hope but also a reminder that life is like the moon. It, too, moves in cycles. In the worst of times, it is important to remember that there will be always be renewal.

The cycles of waxing and waning, of trust and mistrust, of intimacy and distance, of joy and despair, are all normal. A great deal of unhappiness in this world comes from our refusing to acknowledge this simple fact. When things are going well, we want to hold on to those feelings of happiness and bliss. But happiness gives way to sadness, as it surely must. And we suffer needlessly, agonizing over the realization that happiness, once achieved, cannot last forever. In the midst of our disappointment, we forget that the moon will rise again, bringing joy once more.

The great figures of the Bible understood that we need "down" cycles in order to have "up" cycles. Thus, even in the worst of times, they were never immobilized by despair. They used the dark moments to change, to grow, and to move forward.

Women generally seem to understand this concept better than men do. Perhaps this is because feminine physiology is so closely tied to the twenty-eight-day cycle. It is not surprising that in many cultures the moon is a feminine symbol.

Furthermore, women, perhaps better than men, seem to understand the need for taking time off, for setting time aside for regeneration and renewal. (Dr. Clarissa Pinkola Estés, in *Women Who Run with the Wolves,* describes exceptionally well the evolution of this feminine sensitivity from ancient to modern times.)

At this particular juncture in the Bible—a time of war and destruction, when masculine powers are clashing—the moon, a symbol of the feminine, is introduced, bringing with it nurturing, caring, and sensitivity.

It is significant that at this time God tells Moses to instruct the people to pay particular attention to the symbolism of the moon, saying, *"This renewal shall mark for you the beginning of renewals, it shall be the first of the months of the year for you."*

What can this mean? God is clearly saying, "From this moment on, you start a calendar. From this moment on, time begins."

During the Israelites' enslavement in Egypt, their time was not their own. They and their time belonged to their masters. From now on, they would be free. They would be the masters of their own time.

Most of us today, even though we are not slaves, feel that we are not masters of our time. We feel as if time controls us, not the other way around. It's time to go to bed, time to get up, time to pay this year's estimated taxes. To the extent that we allow time to control us, we are still slaves in Egypt—our own Egypt.

It is fascinating that the Hebrew word for "Egypt," *Mitzrayim,* comes from the root *tzar,* meaning "narrow, dangerous place."

Are you in a time tunnel, running like a rat in a maze? If you are, change is necessary. Only when you take charge of your time will you be a free person. That is what the Bible tells us.

As a hospital chaplain, I have been at the bedsides of hundreds of dying patients. I have heard them utter many words of regret—

they wished they had spent more time with their families, they wished they had spent more time appreciating nature, they wished they could have had the opportunity to relive portions of their lives and do things differently. But no one, not one single soul, has ever said to me, "I feel bad that I didn't spend more time at the office."

One particularly poignant incident that I remember involved an elderly man who had undergone hip replacement surgery that proved more complicated than anticipated. He did not come out of anesthesia, remaining in a coma for days while his wife and daughter kept vigil at his bedside. I walked in as his daughter was talking to him softly, stroking his limp hand, saying, "I love you." She looked at me with tears in her eyes. "I'm ashamed to admit," she said, "that I spend more time with my father now that he is in a coma than I did when he was healthy and able to respond. And—" she broke down, sobbing, "—I can't remember when I ever said 'I love you' to him."

I will never forget those words: "I spend more time with my father now that he is in a coma . . ."

So dear reader, I say to you: Be mindful of your time. Make time for the things that are important. There may not be enough time tomorrow. Be the master of your time, not a slave to it.

And remember that absolute certainty never comes. Absolute clarity does not exist. All life is a cycle, never static, always moving. Life is ambiguity, ambivalence. It is the tension of opposites, contradictions, paradoxes. The essence of life is change. Like the moon, we change: We rise, we grow, we feel big, full of ourselves, but then we falter, we fall, we feel small. Yet, as darkness sets in, we rise again. The Bible tells us that this is how it is. That is the order of the world, ordained by God. It is human to falter and fall, so long as we rise again.

The other thing to remember is that the moon's light is reflected. The moon is pale because it merely reflects the light of a much more powerful source—the sun. We must be aware that the moon—our symbolic guide—depends on something greater to shine. And so do we.

If you recall, in Chapter 1 we talked of the divine light called *ohr*—the light, the energy that preceded the creation of physical light. We discussed the illumination that we are expected to create from the black void of our lives. We can create that light only when we connect with the greater energy that exists beyond us and within us.

The moon, our symbol and our light, has light only because it reflects the sun. The other side of the moon is the shadow side. Each one of us, too, has a shadow side, a darker side. Yet we are loath to admit that. But until we admit that we have a shadow side, we cannot confront it and we cannot shine. This is because we have to spend too much energy covering up, pretending it is not there.

For many of us, the shadow side hides a pain inflicted on us by our parents in childhood. But even though many of us swear, "I won't do to my kids what my parents did to me," somehow it happens. This is because we haven't confronted our shadow side.

This is also why revolutionaries, once they succeed in overthrowing tyrants, always seem to adopt the methods of the very people against whom they revolted. This is why minority groups, once they gain equality, always seem to find another group to disparage in turn. This is why those once oppressed become oppressors after they are freed from their oppression.

However, there is an antidote to the shadow side, as the Bible teaches us in the Book of Exodus, and this is what we take up next.

13

Remembering

THUS FAR, THE BOOK OF EXODUS HAS GIVEN US A MOST graphic picture of a man acting out his shadow side: the pharaoh. Crippled by his insecurities, this man lashes out against an entire people, oppressing them in a particularly cruel, vicious manner. What is the first thing the Bible tells us about this pharaoh? That he has a poor memory. The pharaoh does not remember Joseph.

Now, we could argue that, considering the impact Joseph had on Egypt's survival during the famine, the high position he held, and how meticulous the Egyptians were at recording their history, this new pharaoh's poor memory must be a conscious choice.

And the Israelites are commanded in no uncertain terms to make precisely the opposite choice—*never* to forget. "Remember, you were slaves in Egypt," the Israelites are told, in one way or another, over and over again.

When God introduces Himself to the gathering of Israelites at Mount Sinai, He does not say, "I am the Lord your God, who created Heaven and Earth." He does not say, "I am the Lord your God, who created the mountains and the trees and the birds and the animals—and who created you." Instead, He says, *"I am the Lord your God, who brought you out of the Land of Egypt, the house of bondage."*

This is, in fact, the first of the Ten Commandments. *"I am the Lord your God, who brought you out of the land of Egypt, the house of bondage. You shall have no other gods besides Me."* It is a commandment to worship only one God, and it is a commandment to remember.

Indeed, this idea of memory, of never forgetting, is so important that the concept of "remembering" appears in the Bible no less than 169 times:

"You shall not wrong a stranger . . . for you were strangers in the land of Egypt."

"You shall not oppress a stranger, for you know the feelings of the stranger, having yourselves been strangers in the land of Egypt."

"And remember that you were a slave in the land of Egypt."

"You shall love the stranger as yourself, because you were strangers in the land of Egypt."

If you remember your own oppression, your own servitude, your own pain, you will not be able to inflict the same thing on others. That memory will endow you with empathy and compassion—the essential ingredients of love.

Remember the pain and agony. Remembering will motivate you to help others in the same situation. Remember the bad things and put them to good use.

A fellow hospital chaplain once told me that shortly after he graduated from college, he was in a serious car accident. It was a devastating experience for him. At the time he could see no good in it. Only later, when he became a hospital chaplain, did the reason for the accident become evident. He remembered what it felt like to hurt, what it felt like to be immobilized in a hospital bed, what it felt like to be totally dependent on doctors and nurses. He remembered and used that experience in a positive way. He tells me that as a result of his accident, he is able to identify with his patients more fully and to be more compassionate and empathic: "Before the accident, I was not ready to be a chaplain. Before the accident, I could not have truly understood the meaning of illness or hospitalization."

An exemplary volunteer in my department has also chosen to remember the tragedy in his life in a truly inspirational way. He is an amazing human being. When you speak to him, you would never guess the depth of suffering he has endured. A very successful businessman, this man is a Holocaust survivor. And just because he does not wear his painful history on his sleeve does not mean he has forgotten. He has simply chosen to remember in such a way as to make something positive of his memory.

Every Passover, he opens a chest that holds his memories of suffering, and he extracts the concentration camp prisoner's uniform that he wore on the day of his liberation. He has saved it all these years. And each Passover eve, he puts it on. As he retells his children and grandchildren the story of the Israelites' suffering in and redemption from Egypt, that uniform tells them that he also suffered and that he, too, was saved. His point made, he returns the death camp uniform to its chest, puts on a handsome suit—symbolic of the good things in his life—and then sings the Passover songs of liberation and redemption.

As you might guess, he is a man full of empathy for others, a man with a generous heart. I believe this is partly because he has taken the commandment to remember so fully to heart. He remembers that he was once in a narrow, dangerous place and that a lot of people are having similar experiences, on some level, in today's world.

To be homeless is to be in such a situation. Yet how do we look at and respond to homeless people? Do we remember that we, too, were once in a narrow and dangerous place? If we can remember, we won't turn away.

While working on this very chapter, I happened to be walking along a busy Los Angeles street when I saw a homeless man holding up a sign in the direction of passing cars: I AM SURE ALL OF YOU HAVE BEEN NEEDY ONCE IN YOUR LIFE. That is the message of the Bible.

Egypt was once needy, and Joseph came to its aid. But when Egypt was no longer needy, the pharaoh did not remember. People who do not have a memory are like the pharaoh. Unfortunately, there are too many pharaohs in our world. Our tendency, as soon as we manage to rise above poverty or other handicaps that have held us back, is to forget our lowly beginnings. This same tendency is also seen in our desire to shove bad things under the rug, to pretend that our moon has no shadow side, as we discussed in the last chapter.

As a hospital chaplain, I have had the opportunity to see the shadow side of many people, as the hospital is a place that tends to strip one's character to its essence. Nothing brings the shadow side into focus better than the threat of impending death.

Often before people go into surgery, they ask to make a confession. And the things that people are moved to confess are sometimes serious transgressions. They want to unburden themselves of ugly secrets they have not told anyone else, things they hide on their shadow side. Sometimes they see me as an intermediary with God with whom they can bargain for another chance. They promise to make amends with those whom they have hurt, to change their lives for the better.

Of course, most of these people come out of anesthesia to find that the surgery has been successful, and the thing they feared the most has not happened. They've made it. They're alive! Suddenly, the incentive to beg forgiveness and change is gone. But now the chaplain knows their terrible secret.

This is when I find these nice people acting like a pharaoh toward me. Either they pretend the confession never happened or they are angry with me. In that moment of their need, I was seen as their means of salvation; now, I am a reminder of a shadow side that they want to pretend does not exist.

One man confessed to me, right before undergoing complicated heart surgery, that he had been responsible for the untimely death of his mother. He felt he had mistreated her, causing the deep depression that had ultimately led to her death. When this man recovered, he severed his previously friendly relationship with me. This was most unfortunate. In his confession, he had begun to confront his shadow side. If he had chosen to *remember* that, he might have continued the process of acknowledging his shadow. Perhaps his feelings of guilt, if examined in the light of all the facts, were exaggerated. Perhaps he had been acting cruelly toward his mother because of deep-seated hurt inflicted upon him by her. Perhaps his actions had been wrong and selfish and cruel, but his feelings of guilt demonstrated that he had recognized this, that he had indeed changed. Perhaps his confrontation with his shadow side would have led him to forgive himself for what he had done, allowing him to go on with a much lighter burden. By acting like pharaoh, this man denied himself this opportunity.

His behavior is all too human. And we see this exact pattern in the Bible. After repeatedly being told to remember, remember, remember, the Israelites promptly forget. By a remarkable series of miracles, they have been freed from bondage. God has been with them all the way. But now that the vast wilderness is spreading out before them and the pharaoh's army is in pursuit, they forget. They forget how bad things were in Egypt—just a few days ago! Now they say, *"It is better for us to serve the Egyptians than to die in the wilderness."*

God grants them another miracle. They escape the Egyptian pursuit by crossing the Sea of Reeds, but now the water they find is bitter, not fit for drinking. Again they grumble, and again another miracle is granted. Moses casts a tree into the water, rendering it sweet.

But a month later all those miracles are forgotten when they travel farther, again finding no water. Now they say, *"Would that we died . . . in the land of Egypt, when we sat by the flesh-pots, when we did eat bread to the full."*

The lesson here is a simple one. Miracles never sustain faith. As soon as a miracle has been granted, resolving an immediate problem, the attitude of the recipient becomes "What have you done for me lately?" It was true back then, and it is true now. This is because freedom is difficult to handle. We are not truly free until we accept the responsibility that comes with freedom.

The Israelites are physically free. But their mentality remains that of slaves. As slaves, they may have been oppressed, they may have been downtrodden, but they didn't have the burden of being responsible for themselves. The "benefit" of their slavery was that they didn't have to provide for themselves; they didn't have to *think* for themselves. Now they must. Suddenly this freedom, which carries with it the freedom to make choices and to live by the consequences of those choices, is a burden they'd rather not bear.

Freedom is a frightening prospect, so frightening that some would rather be slaves—beaten and reviled—than take on this responsibility.

But at this juncture, another miracle happens. God grants the Israelites a set of basic rules by which to live, rules that will help them make the right choices. These principles of life are designed to sustain a good and moral people, to bring sanctity into everyday life, and to shine like a beacon of good in a world crowded with evil. These are the principles we know as the Ten Commandments.

14

The Ten Commandments

O N THE THIRD DAY, AS MORNING DAWNED, THERE WAS
*thunder, and lightning, and a dense cloud upon the mountain, and a very
loud blast of the horn; and all the people who were in the camp trembled.
Moses led the people out of the camp toward God, and they took their places
at the foot of the mountain."*

In this dramatic way, the Bible sets the stage for that momentous occasion, the giving of the Ten Commandments. Forming the Israelites' code of behavior, this amazing document has since become the basis for ethical behavior throughout much of the world.

Both religious and secular scholars have written volumes about this unique text, and while a wide range of opinions exists, one thing is clear: The Ten Commandments, delivered about 3,200 years ago, represented a breakthrough in the thinking of humankind.

Although a number of ancient law codes predated the Ten Commandments, these earlier codes did *not* include the theoretical idea that binds the Ten Commandments together: namely, that *every* human being is created in the divine image and is unique. The most famous of the ancient legal systems, the Code of Hammurabi, for example, made a distinction between the value of the life of a wealthy man and the life of a poor man. In the Ten Commandments, every human being counts equally.

But the Ten Commandments go further, telling us that God doesn't just care about how we act toward God; God cares about how we act toward one another. That distinguishes the Ten Commandments from all previous legal codes. This message is conveyed succinctly and directly in thirteen short sentences. Yet tradition teaches that "the entire Torah can be found in the Ten Commandments."

That is an astonishing statement. But if we were to examine all the laws and prescriptions for behavior mentioned in the entire Bible, we would find that all of them can be seen as adjuncts or amplifications of these ten basic laws. So let's take a fresh look at this famous document.

It begins, as we might recall from the last chapter, this way: *"I am the Lord your God, who brought you out of the land of Egypt, the house of bondage. You shall have no other gods besides Me."*

If we consider this statement carefully, we see that this first commandment does not regulate actions or words—it does not tell us to do something, nor does it prohibit us from saying something. It is concerned with thought. It is concerned with how we think about and view God.

Many people whom I visit in the hospital begin the conversation with "Rabbi, I have to tell you, I am not a religious person." By this they mean that they do not attend a synagogue or church regularly or that they have divorced themselves from outward religious practice—the do's and don'ts they equate with religion. But they totally forget that an essential part of religion—indeed, the very first commandment—is not the *external* observance but the *internal* thought process.

The First Commandment is, in fact, a call to accept an intensely unique concept of God—a "personal" God: *"I am the Lord your God . . ."*

As we noted earlier, He does not say, "I am the great creator of the moon and stars and the earth" but "I am your liberator." In other words, He is saying, "I saw your suffering and I heard your cries . . . I care when you hurt."

If you are experiencing your own kind of "slavery" in the modern world, the First Commandment is a promise that if you make God your personal God, He will take you out of your personal house of bondage. He will lead you from the narrow and dangerous place of your oppression, just as surely as He led the Israelites out 3,200 years ago.

For all of us, life is fraught with many difficulties created by forces beyond our control—parents, siblings, children, employers, finances, illness, death. But the more we make God our personal God, the more decidedly we break free of whatever is oppressing us.

A patient, a woman dying of cancer, brought this message home to me quite vividly. I was visiting with her, comforting her in her distress, and she was sobbing loudly. At one point she choked out, "There is no more hope."

"Why do you say that?" I asked her.

"There is no cure for this . . . there is no cure for my cancer."

She was right; there was no cure. But the absence of a cure does not mean that there is no hope. A cure may not be possible, but healing is absolutely possible. It happens when we make God our personal God, thus transforming our illness into a new journey and changing our understanding of our life and our goals.

Where does this healing take place? Only in our minds, hearts, or souls. This is why the First Commandment is a commandment of thought, not of action or words.

In contrast, the Second Commandment is a commandment of action, or rather a commandment prohibiting a specific action: *"You shall not make for yourself a graven image . . ."* The Third Commandment is a commandment of words, prohibiting a specific type of speech: *"You shall not swear falsely . . ."* The Fourth Commandment is again a commandment of action, prescribing *"Remember the Sabbath day, to keep it holy . . ."* So in the first four commandments, all the human possibilities and expressions are addressed: thought, speech, and action.

If we examine the remaining six commandments, we see that four of them prescribe or prohibit action: *"Honor your father and your mother. . . . You shall not murder. You shall not commit adultery. You shall not steal."* Then there is another commandment related to words: *"You shall not bear false witness . . ."* The very last commandment, the Tenth Commandment, is again concerned with thought: *"You shall not covet . . ."*

The Bible is stating very clearly that thought, speech, and action are interrelated. While I believe that these three are equally important, I find it particularly intriguing that the first and last commandments are concerned with thought. It is clear that the Bible is saying that all behavior ultimately emanates from thoughts and images.

This is an important biblical theme that is amplified in many other proscriptions that appear throughout the Bible. For example, in the third of the Five Books of Moses, Leviticus, we are told, *"You shall not hate your brother in your heart."*

Hate is a tremendous waste of energy. It brings on all sorts of negative consequences in daily life: You are irritable, snap at your spouse, yell at your children, kick your dog. But even more important, an accumulation of hate leads to hateful action. While it might not necessarily lead to murder, it could lead to a prolonged family feud involving many family members, or it could be the catalyst for our current favorite way of unleashing hate—litigation.

The point is that destructive action begins with destructive thought. No one just commits adultery on a Wednesday evening. The path that eventually leads to adultery starts with unresolved anger toward one's spouse or uncontained desire. An obsession with money will eventually cause one to steal, as the sixteenth-century Bible commentator, Obadiah ben Jacob Sforno, has pointed out. Indeed, the Ten Commandments make it very clear that unbridled yearnings can lead to the violation of the other commandments related to speech and action.

This is why the Tenth Commandment so specifically lists many types of desired items that might get us into trouble: *"You shall not covet your neighbor's house; you shall not covet your neighbor's spouse, or his male or female slave, or his ox or his donkey, or anything that is your neighbor's."*

The coveted items really comprise only three categories: house, spouse, and possessions. You might say that a house is also a possession, but I don't think that this is what the Bible means. A house is much more than that. A house is a symbol of one's most basic security: It is a roof that protects us from the harsh elements of nature, a bed that provides a peaceful night's sleep.

But here the Bible is saying that whatever manner of shelter has been granted to you is good enough. Do not covet the shelter that has been granted to your neighbor. Separate yourself from those thoughts that prod you to get a bigger, nicer place, or you will lose the security that really matters: inner security.

A friend once told me the story of her struggle with this issue. She had purchased a home that she considered second best to what she really wanted. The home that she really wanted, that she considered perfect for all her needs, had not been for sale. She learned that this perfect home was owned by a newly widowed woman living alone, and she reasoned that it would come onto the market in a couple of years. While she waited, she regarded the home in which she lived as only a temporary dwelling. The investments she made in its maintenance were all calculated on the premise that she would not be there very long. She might have made this place more comfortable for herself, but why spend the money? She took frequent walks to look at the "home of her dreams," imagining it hers, with a new paint job, a new fence.

One day, as she was entertaining friends who were saying complimentary things about her current home, she found herself saying, "Ah, but this is nothing, the house I really covet . . ."

The word she unconsciously chose—"covet"—startled her. It reminded her of the Bible, in particular the Tenth Commandment. She then realized what she was doing: wasting a lot of mental energy and preventing herself from enjoying what she already had. "I'm glad I caught myself. If I had gone on in that vein, I don't know what would have happened. I might have started to fantasize about the death of my neighbor. . . . I might have tried to manipulate things so that she would consider putting the house on the market. . . . I might have done things I would later regret."

She was frank in her self-examination. Most of us are not. We simply get caught up in plotting and planning how we are going to acquire "X," the thing we covet.

The Bible talks about coveting donkeys and slaves, but in modern terms these are equivalent to cars and computers. The problem with coveting any and all possessions is that their acquisition is often an attempt to fill an emptiness inside. But spiritual emptiness cannot be filled with things. If we try to do that, we only find ourselves craving more and bigger things.

How many of us have purchased a state-of-the-art, elaborate computer only to see that a friend's more advanced model makes ours look inferior? Immediately, we are not satisfied with what we have, and we begin to feel that we can't live without the new model.

Some people seem to have this same kind of attitude toward relationships, which contributes greatly to our divorce rate. As soon as the object of their desire loses his or her attraction, they look around for a new model—one more attractive, more understanding, or more exciting.

I do a lot of counseling of men and women in second and third marriages that are based on misplaced desire. Typically, the men desire a younger, more beautiful "trophy" wife whom they can parade before their aging friends. And typically, the women desire the status, wealth, or power that they will gain through a new husband. If it is only desire that connects two people, their marriage will fail. Desire can never be satisfied, and the satisfaction of one yearning is quickly followed by the arising of another.

SO IT IS CLEAR WHY THE BIBLE FORBIDS US TO COVET, TO BECOME ABsorbed and eventually swallowed up by desire for one thing or another. This is also why the Bible is so preoccupied with thought, because every desire begins with a thought that becomes a daydream, a fantasy, an obsession, and so on.

But how do we banish such dangerous thoughts? After all, thoughts usually come to us uninvited; thoughts fly in and out of our heads, triggered by an endless variety of stimuli. More frequently than not, we do not decide what to think; we just seem to be the recipients of thoughts arising from who-knows-where.

We do recognize, however, that some of the thoughts that come our way are good, while others are bad. So what do we do with bad thoughts? What responsibility do we have for something that comes to us unbidden?

We are not responsible for having these thoughts, but we are responsible for how we deal with them. The choice is strictly ours: We can banish them from our mind, we can turn them into something positive, or we can feed them so that they grow and grow, eventually leading to unethical actions.

A famous poem by William Blake, "A Poison Tree," perfectly sums up the consequences of our choices:

> I was angry with my friend:
> I told my wrath, my wrath did end.

I was angry with my foe:
I told it not, my wrath did grow.

Even before an evil action takes place, harm and hurt result. We tend to think of pain in physical terms, as if hurt requires clobbering someone with a hammer. But there are other ways of inflicting pain: Words do it, and so do thoughts.

We've all been in the presence of a person who acts very nice toward us, saying all the right things and bringing us gifts, yet we sense that this person does not really wish us well. We feel it regardless of whatever else is happening on the surface. No one can completely hide what he or she is thinking, and angry feelings have the potential to hurt others as much as angry words or deeds do. This is why the Bible puts thoughts on a par with words and actions, giving them equal—and perhaps even greater—importance.

But what if we have been terribly hurt by someone and find it impossible to banish the angry thoughts that constantly keep creeping into our mind? How can we not be eaten alive by the bitterness and anger that we may justifiably feel? The answer is to transform the negative into something positive.

I am reminded of a play by Christopher Marlowe, *The Tragical History of Doctor Faustus*, and the later two-part tragedy by Johann Wolfgang von Goethe based on the same legend. These dramatists were preoccupied with thoughts of evil incarnate, but they turned them into something positive: a play, a book. Creativity is the answer. Throughout this book, we have repeatedly returned to the theme of creating light out of darkness.

Negative and evil thoughts plunge us into a kind of darkness, but creativity serves to illuminate and dispel that darkness.

Not all of us are playwrights, but the ways in which we can be creative are endless. We can paint, we can adopt hobbies, we can do volunteer work. The key thing is to create something positive with which to displace the negative within us. Is it difficult? Extremely. But we need never feel that we must do it alone. We can have a dialogue with God. We have angels to call upon for help. And we have all manner of advice in the Bible to help us cope, as we shall continue to see in subsequent chapters.

15

A Day of Rest

OST PEOPLE THINK THEY KNOW THE STORY OF
creation. If you were to ask almost anyone, I think they would tell
you that there were six days of creation and that, on the seventh
day, God rested. But that is a superficial reading of the text. In
fact, the Bible says that by the end of the sixth day, *"the heaven and
the earth were finished."* But by no means did God cease to create, because on the seventh day God created *rest.* It is important to keep
in mind that divine energy was used in creating rest.

We tend to think of "rest" as a day off. But rest in the biblical
sense is a continuation of creation. For six days, we create the ex-
ternals; on the seventh day—the Sabbath—we create the internal.
Perhaps this is why the word "recreation" (read: re-creation) has
become so closely associated with the Sabbath day. Regrettably,
today we define recreation as playing softball instead of what it
was meant to be, the refocusing of creative, spiritual energy.

This day of re-creation is of critical importance. Note that of all

the Ten Commandments, the one dealing with the Sabbath day—
the Fourth Commandment—stands out in the number of words it
takes the Bible to communicate the idea. Only the Second Commandment—prohibiting graven images—comes close to being as
long and as specific.

This is what the Fourth Commandment says: *"Remember the Sabbath day to keep it holy. Six days you shall labor and do all your work,
but the seventh day is a Sabbath of the Lord your God; you shall not do
any work—you, your son or daughter, your male or female slave, or your
cattle, or the stranger who is within your settlements. For in six days the
Lord made heaven and earth and sea, and all that is in them, and He
rested on the seventh day; therefore the Lord blessed the Sabbath day and
hallowed it."*

Not only is this commandment longer than the other commandments, its importance is stressed on more than a dozen occasions throughout the Bible. For example, the point is made that
even though it is very important to respect one's parents (the Fifth
Commandment), if there is a conflict between honoring one's parents and honoring the Sabbath, the Sabbath takes precedence.

In another even more dramatic example, as the Israelites prepare
to build a tabernacle for God, they are reminded that even in this
holy endeavor the Fourth Commandment cannot be ignored: *"Six
days shall work be done, but on the seventh day there shall be to you a holy
day, a Sabbath of complete rest to the Lord."*

It couldn't be more clear: if we cannot violate the Sabbath to
build God's house, surely we cannot do so to perform any lesser activity.

In Deuteronomy, during Moses's farewell address to his people,
he again warns, *"Observe the Sabbath day to keep it holy, as the Lord
your God has commanded you. . . . Remember that you were a slave in the
land of Egypt and the Lord your God freed you from there with a mighty
hand and an outstretched arm; therefore the Lord your God has commanded you to observe the Sabbath day."*

Having been solemnly instructed in this manner, the Israelites made a special point of keeping the Sabbath—a unique idea in the history of humankind. Of course, since then the practice of keeping the Sabbath has been adopted by much of the world. Jews observe the Sabbath from sundown on Friday to sundown on Saturday; Christians set aside Sunday for this purpose; and Muslims observe their Sabbath on Friday. However, before the spread of Christianity and Islam, the Israelites (later known as Jews) were the only ones keeping the Sabbath.

When in 330 B.C.E. the Jews were conquered by Greece, this supposedly superior civilization considered the Jewish practice of not working on the Sabbath to be evidence of idleness. The Greeks could not comprehend why anyone would want to "waste" a full seventh of one's life.

With their pursuit of beauty and intellect, the Greeks ignored the pursuit of the spirit. They did not see that the seventh day served to recharge the spirit of the Israelites, giving them fresh energy for the work they would have to do during the course of the following six days.

Many Jewish thinkers have seen the observance of the Sabbath as the key to the survival of the Jewish people in the face of insurmountable odds and relentless persecution. It is the one religious observance—perhaps more than any other—that has rejuvenated them, that has given them strength when all seemed lost.

Numerous philosophers and other prominent thinkers have asked the questions, How did the Jews survive? What is their secret? Leo Tolstoy posed this question. So did Mark Twain. In a *Harper's* magazine article in 1897, Twain wrote:

> If the statistics are right, the Jews constitute but one quarter of one percent of the human race. It suggests a nebulous dim puff of star dust lost in the blaze of the Milky Way. Properly, the Jew ought hardly to be heard of; but he is heard of, has al-

ways been heard of. He is as prominent on the planet as any other people, and his importance is extravagantly out of proportion to the smallness of his bulk.

His contributions to the world's list of great names in literature, science, art, music, finance, medicine and abstruse learning are also very out of proportion to the weakness of his numbers. He has made a marvelous fight in this world in all ages; and has done it with his hands tied behind him. He could be vain of himself and be excused for it. The Egyptians, the Babylonians and the Persians rose, filled the planet with sound and splendor; then faded to dream-stuff and passed away; the Greeks and the Romans followed and made a vast noise, and they are gone; other peoples have sprung up and held their torch high for a time but it burned out, and they sit in twilight now, or have vanished.

The Jew saw them all, survived them all, and is now what he always was, exhibiting no decadence, no infirmities of age; no weakening of his parts, no slowing of his energies, no dulling of his alert and aggressive mind. All things are mortal but the Jew; all other forces pass, but he remains. What is the secret of his immortality?

To this question, Asher Ginzberg, the Zionist thinker better known by his pen name Ahad Ha'am, gave a succinct answer: "More than the Jewish people have kept the Sabbath, the Sabbath has kept the Jewish people." This practice is so deeply ingrained among Jewish people that those who choose to abandon it rapidly feel the consequences.

A Jewish psychologist friend of mine, who for years resisted the pleas of his patients to make himself available on Saturdays, finally decided, "Why not?" He could easily fill his calendar on the day most people had off from work, and he could earn an extra $10,000 a year in the process. Yet as soon as he opened his office on Saturdays, he began to notice that he had less to give during the week. He experienced great fatigue, yet he recognized that it was not entirely physical.

Wistfully, he would watch people walking to a nearby synagogue, people he had hardly paid attention to before. He would see families strolling together, making him acutely aware that he was taking time away from his own family. Within a few months, he realized that working on the Sabbath was not in his best interest.

When telling me this story, he said, "One who doesn't observe the Sabbath experiences a self-annihilation, because he doesn't refurbish his energy." His choice of words reminded me of the warning Moses gives to the Israelites in telling them to keep the Sabbath: *"Six days shall work be done, but on the seventh day there shall be to you a holy day . . . whoever shall do work therein shall be put to death."* This was an awesome thing to say. In addition to its legal meaning, Moses is saying, metaphorically, that by working without pause we kill ourselves.

Of course, we see this phenomenon all around us today. People who cannot manage the stresses of daily life find themselves seriously ill. Heart disease, the number one killer in America, has long been linked to overwork and excessive stress.

Do we have to work that hard? Do we have to work nonstop? Wouldn't it be wonderful if, no matter what religion we are, we chose to set aside one day a week to spend with our families or friends, to enjoy other people, to meditate on our lives, thereby growing closer to God?

The Bible tells us that this is the secret of life. The Ten Commandments tell us that this is an integral part of being. Indeed, we are commanded to live our lives this way.

Yet why do we find it so hard to set aside a day for the God who created us, the God to whom we will one day return?

There is a story, which has been retold often and in many versions, of a person who dies and confronts God. God asks, "Who are you?"

The person answers, "A doctor." (Of course, he or she could just as well be a nurse, an accountant, or a salesperson or any number of other professions, trades, or occupations.)

God persists: "Who are you?"

The person gropes. "I'm an Italian American." (Or an African American or a Frenchman or a Mexican or whatever.)

"Who are you?"

"I'm a husband and father." (Or a wife and mother or a single person.)

"Who are you?"

"I'm Joe." (Or Sarah or David or Jessica.)

"Who are you?"

"I'm lonely." (Or frightened or vulnerable or weak.)

"Who are you?"

Eventually, the person falls silent, because God is really asking, "Who are you in relationship to Me?" And that answer is acquired only through years of pondering, through setting aside one day a week for God, through the questions and answers that come from a dialogue with Him.

But when do we make time for that? The answer is the Sabbath.

Don't do anything for one day. Don't build a temple, don't go shopping, don't pay your bills, don't create physically, don't do anything externally. There is holy inner work to be done, and that requires the cessation of all external activity. Not doing any work is holy! Taking all your energy and focusing it on the internal is holy. There is great power in this practice, as the survival of the Jews demonstrates.

If you feel persecuted by life, chased by bills, oppressed by the demands of your family and work worlds, try this for a day. Stop. Think. Take a walk. Sing a song. See what happens.

I predict that if you do so, God will enter your life, and from then on things will never be the same. When you return to work, you will find a new energy, new purpose for the things you are doing. You will then be experiencing God's promise to Moses—that He has a beautiful gift in His house of treasures, and its name is Sabbath.

16

You Are What You Eat

Y OU MAY HAVE NOTICED THAT THE FOURTH COMMAND-
ment, in its concern that everyone get a day of rest, includes animals: *"You shall not do any work—you, your son or daughter, your male
or female slave, or your cattle."* It may seem peculiar, at first glance,
that God should list cattle in the same sentence as human beings.
However, in the context of the Bible, it is very clear that God has
a deep concern for all He has created.

The Bible lauds those—Rebecca and Moses, for example—who
show kindness to animals. Numerous prescriptions relating to the
treatment of animals are enumerated: for returning a lost animal
(even to one's enemy); for immediately unloading a donkey that
has fallen under its burden; and for plowing so that no undue
hardship is placed on two animals of unequal size. But nowhere is
this concern more paramount than in the various commandments
relating to what we should and should not eat. And these are
found as early as in the Garden of Eden: *"God said, 'See, I give you*

every seed-bearing plant that is upon all the earth, and every tree that has seed-bearing fruit; they shall be yours for food.' " Of course, the tree of knowledge of good and evil is not included, but Adam and Eve are told several different times that they can eat anything else that grows in the Garden.

It is clear that this includes any form of vegetable or plant life. The animals were already created, but there is no reference to them as food. The only things Adam and Eve are given permission to eat are fruits and vegetables.

There are two key thoughts here: that everything God created has some form of life and that man was meant to be a vegetarian. Those of you out there who are vegetarians are probably cheering, and the rest of you may be in shock. Wait; it gets a bit more complicated. Because if we look at the story of Noah, we find that the rules change.

We learn that things have not been going so well since Adam and Eve were expelled from the Garden of Eden. It is written, *"The earth became corrupt before God; the earth was filled with lawlessness."* In fact, things are going so badly that God decides to destroy all He has created in a great flood—all except for the one righteous man, Noah, his family, and the animals that Noah is allowed to save. After the great flood, God gives human beings a second chance, saying to Noah, *"Every creature that lives shall be yours to eat; as with the green grasses, I give you all."*

So we are now given permission to eat every beast, fish, and fowl. Why is this permitted after the flood, when it was clearly not permitted earlier?

I believe that God made a concession to human nature, to people's weaknesses and frailty. There had been some terrible things going on before the flood: murder, incest, all manner of violence and corruption. And God apparently decided that fruits and vegetables were not enough to sustain the primal appetites. Therefore, God now seems to be saying, "I will give you meat to eat, and if you eat meat, perhaps you will be placated, appeased, satisfied."

But in so doing, He sets up a huge paradox with which humanity must grapple. And the paradox is that we must destroy life in order to sustain life.

This also applies to vegetarians, who destroy some kinds of plant life. But destruction of life is perhaps more graphic for meat eaters. All spiritually sensitive people the world over, whether or not they have read the Bible, are on some deep level innately aware of this paradox, and they try to reconcile themselves to it. Buddhists, for example, are vegetarians. Rastafarians go so far as to eat only nuts and fruits that fall to the ground, in order not to damage any form of plant life. Native Americans recite special prayers before hunting and killing animals, even before cutting down trees.

In his book *The Final Forest,* the Pulitzer Prize–winning writer William Dietrich tells a beautiful story about this. He describes how the Native Americans of the Pacific Northwest were required to ask permission of a cedar tree before they could cut it down to make one of their seventy-foot-long canoes. If the image of the canoe did not appear in the bark, it meant that the tree was not willing to give them permission and they would have to continue asking until they found a tree that was willing.

This paradox of killing to live explains, of course, why Jews, Muslims, and others have special dietary laws.

It is also the reason for saying a blessing before a meal. Here we are, sitting in front of a piece of meat—a piece of a slaughtered animal—and before we consume it, we try to sanctify the act somehow. If we say a blessing before we eat, the whole activity of eating doesn't take on the base posture of satisfying our appetite, our lust for food. Also, it is hoped, we will eat with moderation, being aware of how much we are removing from the food chain.

We are reminded of this and of the value of animal life through a proscription that appears at this juncture in the Book of Exodus, after the giving of the Ten Commandments: *"You shall not boil a kid in its mother's milk."* Apparently, the pagans of the day enjoyed this particular treat. But the Bible says that only a barbarian of the worst sort would take a baby animal away from its mother, heartlessly empty her udders, and then use the milk *and* the baby, for which the milk was intended, to prepare a delicacy for himself. The Bible asks, How much can you take from the food chain? How much is enough? Is there no limit to decadence at the expense of other living creatures?

Because of this passage, Jews take care not to eat meat and dairy products together, an aspect of keeping "kosher." But even those who are not Jewish cannot ignore the obvious message that it makes a great deal of difference how we kill our food and how we consume what we kill.

This idea has yet another level of meaning, which we can discern from a commandment given to Noah: *"You must not, however, eat flesh with its lifeblood in it."*

As plain as day, this says that you can eat certain animals, fish and fowl, but not with their blood. How can that be? Is there not blood in all flesh? What kind of Catch-22 is this?

Well, it clearly means that you cannot eat a living animal. The Bible commentator Rashi notes that this prohibition has a double significance: Cruelty to animals is forbidden, and so is partaking of their blood, since it is the core of life.

Unlike a lion, which chases and catches a gazelle, you cannot start ripping the limbs off a living creature and stuffing them into your mouth on the spot, with the blood dripping down your chin. That would be pretty barbaric. Much more than that is expected from a human being.

This point is driven home repeatedly. Ripping and tearing limbs and spilling blood to be eaten is somehow inhuman. So that this will be crystal clear, it is reiterated later: *"And you must not consume any blood, either of bird or of animal, in any of your settlements. Anyone who eats blood shall be cut off from his kin."* Why should consuming animal blood be such a terrible transgression?

It is not so strange. Consider what it means to call a person "bloodthirsty." When we use that word to describe someone, we mean to point out—and quite graphically, too—that this individual is a lover of violence and killing.

I was fascinated to learn about the food practices of the Masai tribe in Kenya, who tend cattle and basically exist on plants and eggs. When the Masai prepare to go to war, they eat meat and drink a potion made of blood. They believe that this prepares them for the killing that will be necessary.

This notion of linking blood—red meat, if you will—to aggression and violence also finds its source in the Bible. The idea is that human beings have a proclivity to violence and evil. There is a part of them that is good and soulful, but there is also a part that is base and primal. And these different aspects are in constant struggle. If a man consumes blood, he is quite literally feeding the primal aspect of himself, thus intensifying his primal side and complicating the conflict within himself.

If you find this a difficult concept, consider the basic law of physics, which we took up in the very first chapter—that energy cannot be destroyed, only transformed. We know that calories represent the energy value of food. We consume food—that is, calories—to acquire the energy we need to accomplish the tasks of our life, and if we eat meat, we are consuming animal energy.

Why do football players eat steak for breakfast when in training? Because it gives them energy; it hones their aggressive instincts; it makes them fight harder on the field. Or so their coaches tell them.

The Bible is saying the same thing: If you eat in a certain way, you will have a greater tendency to act accordingly. On a deeper level, it is really talking about the struggle within, the struggle between the two parts of ourselves: the primal and the soulful.

The Bible recognizes and responds to the paradoxical nature of human beings. And it tells us that we can eat meat—to feed the primal parts of ourselves—but we must take care as to *how* we do it, so as not to feed our primal blood lust. In the modern world, rarely does anyone pay attention to "how" we do it. Perhaps this is due in part to the fact that seldom does the average person get to witness the slaughtering of an animal. This is done far away from us, in a place we shudder to imagine if we think about it at all. When we buy meat in a store, it is neatly wrapped in cellophane or glossy white paper or attractively packaged in a jar of spaghetti sauce. The symbolism of violence, blood, and flesh has been removed from our awareness.

As we have seen, symbols have enormous power to bring the abstract into consciousness, and some people are very aware of that. A colleague of mine who is a vegetarian has an arresting picture hanging in her kitchen. It is a reproduction of a Marc Chagall painting, *Le Boeuf Écorché,* which depicts a skinned animal hanging by its legs while its blood drains into a bucket.

When I first saw it, I was shocked. "Why?" I asked.

"It's to not forget," she said. She then pointed to a small figure of a biblical-looking prophet, hardly noticeable in the corner of the painting. "I read that Chagall put him there to proclaim the terrible truth that it takes the bloody sacrifice of the innocent to make us see the need for love and peace."

To her, this dramatic picture serves as a symbolic reminder of the violence and death of war, of the Holocaust, of places such as Bosnia and Rwanda, and of the slums in American cities where gang warfare too often claims the lives of the innocent. When one is protected by the security of a comfortable home and loving family, the evil remains somewhere outside, far away, too easily forgotten or ignored. Yet it's there, part of a struggle that continues to be played out every day—the struggle between the soulful and primal parts of us.

THIS STRUGGLE IS PLAYED OUT NOT ONLY IN VIOLENCE BUT ALSO IN another primal drive: sex.

Recently a woman came to me for therapy because she was deeply troubled about the sexual aspects of her marriage. Her complaint was one I have heard from numerous other female clients. She was not complaining that her husband had a mistress, nor was she feeling sexually neglected. Rather, in describing her sexual relationship with her spouse, she used words that one might use to describe a rape. She was saying quite plainly that sex, as she experienced it in her marriage, was not a blissful union but a violation.

As she did the hard work of therapy, she was able to discover that what dominated her marriage was lust, which is the more primal form of sex, as contrasted with love, the more soulful form of sex. When women or men feel violated during sexual intercourse, it is because they have experienced the lust without the soul. Unfortunately, I hear this complaint frequently in therapy sessions, especially from women.

This particular client's marriage ended in divorce. As she learned the meaning of real love, she realized that it had never been present in her relationship with her husband; lust had dominated their union from the start.

Another case still troubles me deeply. A couple came to see me for marriage counseling. Both were attractive, intelligent, professional people in their forties, and I could not immediately discern the problem. It started to become clear to me only when I had a series of sessions with each of them separately. The wife complained that the husband (whom she called "an ignoramus") had lost sexual interest in her. The husband acknowledged that this was so, saying that he found his wife—who was a most attractive woman by any standard—no longer sexually appealing because she was flat-chested.

Note that the husband had not had a stroke or any injury that would have diminished his intelligence during the course of their marriage. Note also that the wife had not had breast reduction surgery that would have diminished her proportions after they were married. What had diminished was their respect for each other.

After a while, I began to wonder if there had ever been much respect at all. The wife had always viewed the husband as a financial security blanket; the husband viewed the wife as a body—he was having sex with a body, not a person. Lust had carried them along for a while, but now that its veneer had grown thin, these people were wondering why they were together.

The situations I see are not always that bleak. Often there is real love in a marriage, but if both partners are not careful to nurture it, love can wither away and lust can take over. It is so much easier to treat the person in bed next to you—with all of his or her needs, wants, problems, and complications—simply as a body. The urge to satisfy our primal physical needs comes to us naturally; it is the stronger drive within us.

But it would be a mistake to suggest that the soulful part is shy or fragile or retiring. If we allow the primal part to win, our soul lets us know. This is when we experience guilt, frustration, anxiety, and depression. These forces—lust on the one side and a craving toward divinity on the other—are in constant conflict. And this struggle is difficult.

Indeed, it is no accident that so many ancient religions had sacred prostitutes. In some cases, they were a way of venerating and paying tribute to man's primal side; in others, they were an attempt to sanctify and contain the sexual drive by dedicating it to the service of the gods. Some religions have dealt with this issue by going in the opposite direction and suppressing sex, or at least putting severe limitations on it.

Whatever the approach, it would be fair to say that no religion or society has escaped the struggle. It's no easy matter, and the Bible is reminding us of this fact. It is telling us to be aware that these two forces coexist, causing us continuing conflict. I would venture to say that most people recognize this but have tremendous difficulty dealing with it. Too bad we don't have a blessing before sex as we do before meals. But considering the complex nature of human sexuality, a blessing wouldn't be enough. Your marriage, your relationship, your life must be like a blessing in all aspects; only then can the blessing materialize in the bedroom as well.

We shall shortly examine the tremendous amount of advice that the Bible gives us about sex, love, and marriage. But before we get to that, we have some other basic needs to explore.

17

Sanctuary

SINCE THE EARLIEST CHAPTERS OF GENESIS, WE HAVE SEEN that the relationship between God and humankind is a highly interactive one. At every juncture, God is sensitive to the struggles of human beings, whom He has created and endowed with free choice.

After He creates Adam, God sees that the first man is lonely, and He responds to his need by creating a companion for him.

Having destroyed most of the warring world in a flood, God promises that He will not do so again. He rescinds the prohibition against the eating of animal flesh, with the apparent hope that this might assuage man's passion for violence.

When Abraham challenges God over the imminent fate of Sodom and Gomorrah, God responds to Abraham's argument, agreeing to spare the cities if ten good men can be found.

He grants signs to Abraham, Jacob, Joseph, and Moses that aid and inspire them in times of struggle.

Understanding fully the emotional fragility of the newly liberated slaves, God presents them with miracle after miracle during their flight from Egypt.

And at Mount Sinai, in giving the Ten Commandments, God again responds to the need of His creatures by providing them with a tangible symbol of His presence among them—a sanctuary.

Until now, we have seen that the great figures of the Bible could commune with God just about anywhere. In a world abounding with pagan monoliths and edifices erected to all manner of gods, the followers of the God of the Bible are unique in seeking Him in the wilderness, rather than in a temple. Indeed, the patriarchs most often encounter God in remote settings and in solitude. But in a community, such solitude is not always possible. One cannot abandon one's function in a larger society and run off for a month of communing with God in the forest or in the mountains. The shepherds are lucky in this regard, but what about the others?

Furthermore, the Israelites have just come from a society that is very visually oriented; they have been socialized to need tangible representations of the intangible. In Egypt, they were surrounded by pyramids, sphinxes, and mammoth representations of the deities. Yet here in the desert, they are specifically forbidden to make a graven image.

Still, as always, God is sensitive to their needs. He summons Moses to the top of Mount Sinai again, commanding him to tell the Israelites to build a symbol of His presence among them: *"Build for Me a sanctuary so that I may dwell among them."* The Bible lists specific requirements as to how this sanctuary is to be constructed, how the Ark of the Covenant, which is to contain the stone tablets of the Ten Commandments, is to be shaped and adorned, and how offerings are to be made within this sanctuary. God's instructions to Moses anticipate the great sin of the Israelites that is about to take place.

While Moses is on the mountaintop with God for forty days, the people down below are growing restless. Their leader has been gone too long, their God is invisible, and their craving for something they can see and touch becomes overwhelming.

We can well empathize with the Israelites at Sinai, since we also live in a society addicted to visual representations of the intangible. Do we not want to capture every special moment in a snapshot or a home movie? Have we not gradually abandoned reading as a form of recreation in favor of motion pictures and videos? Do we not measure success—and, all too often, our worth and the worth of others—by the material manifestations of that success?

We are also a people who yearn for the concrete. Although we want to hear "I love you," the words begin to fall on deaf ears if our beloved never gives them tangible meaning by his or her acts. "I love you" has to translate into thoughtfulness, emotional support, and, even more important, tangible proofs of that love. Do we not prize those greeting cards, sent on no special occasion, which just say "I love you"? Do we not save and treasure those unique gifts that concretize the words of love within a symbol of a heart or a message engraved on a piece of jewelry?

The Israelites have just made a covenant with God. They have heard the giving of the Ten Commandments with their own ears, but only weeks later, the memory of that experience has waned. It needs to be symbolized somehow. So they erect a golden calf.

They know full well the symbolism of such a statue. The pagan peoples of the Middle East have long worshiped the god Baal, represented as a bull. The Egyptians worship the goddess Hathor, represented as a cow or a woman with cow horns.

The rest, as they say, is history. Moses comes down from the mountain, smashing the tablets of the Ten Commandments in a rage. Rallying the tribe of Levi around him, he brings order to the camp and then asks God to forgive the people.

But God is reluctant. He grants forgiveness, promising the Israelites success in future endeavors, but He withholds His presence, saying, *"But I will not go in your midst, since you are a stiff-necked people."*

Moses goes up the mountain yet again, renewing the covenant and continuing to plead with God to be present among the people. In the dialogue that ensues, God relents little by little. In an exchange reminiscent of God's discourse with Abraham prior to the destruction of Sodom, God is gradually convinced.

Eventually, a reconciliation is reached, completing a cycle that we have seen repeated over and over in the dealings between God and humans: the development of trust, followed by betrayal, followed by reconciliation and the establishment of a higher level of trust based on a new awareness. As a symbol of this new relationship, the sanctuary is built of the finest materials the Israelites possess.

At this juncture it is important to remember that the sanctuary was not meant to be a house that *contained* God. God did *not* say, "Build for Me a sanctuary so that I may dwell *in it.*" God said, *"Build for Me a sanctuary so that I may dwell among them."* The sanctuary is only a symbol. But it serves as a powerful physical reminder of His presence.

THUS FAR, THE SYMBOLS PRESENTED BY GOD HAVE BEEN NATURAL ones (as we discussed in Chapter 12), such as a tree, a rainbow, a rock, the moon. But now God, recognizing the human need to touch and hold, allows the creation of a man-made symbol. This is why synagogues are so important to Jews, churches to Christians, and mosques to Muslims. Indeed, most cultures have concretized the presence of God amid man by erecting elaborate edifices.

The danger with any symbol, of course, is that in time people tend to worship the symbol, forgetting that it is meant only to be a reminder of our ongoing process of spiritual development. And no wonder. Isn't it easier to go to a synagogue on Saturday or a church on Sunday, feeling that one's religious obligation has thus been fulfilled, than to relate to those symbols as aids in one's spiritual growth?

Some so-called religious people make a great show of their

weekend religious observance, yet they simultaneously inflict hurt on their families, cheat on their taxes, and act ruthlessly in their business dealings with the very strangers they are commanded to love. They forget that we are meant to seek God within the sanctuary so that we may be more fully aware of Him in our midst throughout the week. The symbols we substitute for reality need not only be houses of worship, of course. We are capable of corrupting all kinds of symbols.

One of my Bible class students, a member of the hospital's geriatric committee, confessed to me that while hurrying to a committee meeting, he had ignored the plight of an elderly person he encountered. Only later had he realized that he was more comfortable with the symbolic representations of his position and the *abstract* issues of aging than the nitty-gritty of actually helping an elderly person in need. This is also an example of a symbol becoming an idol. The spirit behind the representation has been lost.

That is not to say that symbols always degenerate into idols. A symbol is doing its work when it allows our spirit to soar, when it brings forth feelings with which we want to connect, when it allows our religious imagination to blossom.

Indeed, the world is replete with all kinds of religious symbols, and I can readily see the sustenance these symbols offer. Although I am a Jewish chaplain, patients of other faiths sometimes seek my counsel. A Christian man, prior to undergoing surgery, shared with me what the cross he was holding in his hand meant to him. He saw the intersection of the vertical with the horizontal as an illustration of the vertical relationship between man on earth and God up in heaven, and the horizontal relationships that human beings have with one another. "Rabbi," he said, "these two types of relationships must intersect." I agreed with him.

For Jews, the Star of David often serves as a source of comfort. Gershom Scholem points out that it is made of two intersecting triangles, one pointing upward to heaven, the other downward. Scholem suggests that the ascending triangle symbolizes the good inclination of man and the descending triangle symbolizes the evil inclination. Man exists where they intersect.

The chapel of the hospital where I work as chaplain features a prominent Star of David with the emblem of the medical profession—the caduceus—at its center. The two symbols together are meant to remind all who see them of the Divine Presence in healing, of the combined strength of human skills and the Ultimate Healer.

A symbol can be a powerful thing. It can remind us of our connection to God and inspire special feelings within us. We somehow feel better by looking at it or touching it. Of course, I must admit that in my experience I have seen people choose some pretty unusual symbolic representations of things they consider important.

Early in my chaplaincy, I visited a patient, an unmarried woman in her forties who was dying of cancer. By her bed sat a huge stuffed animal, a black gorilla. This gorilla was her protector, keeping away the frightening creatures of the night. She even asked that the gorilla be buried with her when she died.

More commonly, patients bring in less dramatic symbols; it is not unusual, for example, to see small stuffed animals, particularly teddy bears, sharing patients' beds. At the moment when their illnesses cause them to lose control over their lives and to be dependent on others, these patients cling to a child's security symbol. I hasten to add that by no means do I consider patients with toys to be overgrown children. Toys can be symbols of healing in a positive sense.

I know of a woman in her thirties—I shall call her "Anne"— who, after experiencing several early miscarriages, found herself well along into pregnancy. She knew the child would be a girl; she planned to name her Lila. Somewhere along the way, as she gradually began to buy small things for the baby, she purchased a tiny teddy bear wearing a lilac wool sweater.

Then tragedy struck. An ultrasound examination found a serious deformity in the fetus. After undergoing numerous tests and examinations, Anne and her husband had to face the fact that their baby stood no chance of surviving. It was expected to die long before birth, and it would endanger Anne's life. A therapeutic abortion was the only solution.

Anne was heartbroken. In her grief, she found great solace in hugging the tiny teddy bear in its little lilac sweater. After so many months of hope, followed by anxiety, tragedy, and grieving, the teddy bear was the only tangible symbol of this baby that could not live.

I know this is a heartbreaking story, but we can take comfort in the knowledge that God understands the depths of our grief perfectly. He sends us symbols of solace. And with Him in our midst, we can always find a sanctuary for our tears.

PART III

18

Coming Closer

WE ARE NOW READY TO BEGIN THE THIRD OF THE FIVE Books of Moses. In Hebrew, this book is named *Vayyikra,* after its opening, *"And God called to Moses . . ."* He called to Moses unexpectedly. God did not make an appointment with Moses. He did not say, "Be here Tuesday at 3:00 P.M." He called to Moses out of the blue, so to speak. And indeed this is how God more often than not confronts us: His call might be direct or oblique, but it is bound to come when we least expect it.

At a time most inconvenient, there comes that tap on the shoulder: "Brother, can you spare a dime?" This usually happens on a day when you have only enough change for the bus. You are late for an important meeting, speeding down the highway, when you see an elderly woman standing helplessly next to a disabled vehicle. The thought goes through your mind that this is one of those "love your neighbor" situations, but stopping might mean losing that business deal.

It's almost guaranteed. If you were feeling particularly loving to humanity, cruising the streets looking for a person in need, you would probably have a hard time finding one. Acts of kindness or heroism, and those special opportunities to answer the call, don't come when you are well prepared, as this opening passage of *Vayyikra* suggests.

In English, *Vayyikra* is known as Leviticus, named after the tribe of Levi, whose members, the priests, supervised the rituals in the sanctuary and, later, in the Temple. Thus, *Vayyikra*/Leviticus represents the call to come closer to God through the means of various rituals and sacrifices. (It is interesting that the Hebrew word *korban,* often mistranslated as "sacrifice," comes from the root *karev,* meaning "to come closer to God.")

A lot of people who read the Book of Leviticus get lost in the details or are put off by the talk of animal sacrifice. They see these laws as meant for ancient, more primitive peoples and irrelevant to today's world. But it has to be kept in mind that in the ancient world of the Israelites, sacrifices of animals, birds, or foodstuffs were external manifestations of the desire to relate to God. Along with the sacrifices, the people also offered meditations, reflections, and prayers.

Of course, no one has taken turtledoves or flour cakes to the Temple in some 2,000 years, not since the Romans destroyed Jerusalem. But the prayers remain, and the reason they are offered, with or without sacrifice, is as relevant today as it was in ancient times.

When we read these passages in Leviticus, we see that the sacrifices were intended to represent all manner of human feeling and behavior. Thus, the Bible tells us that religion is linked to every aspect of life.

All too often, people make the mistake of trying to separate the ritual observance of religion from life, as if ritual observance can be compartmentalized and separated from human feelings and behavior. Of course, secular people simply dismiss the ritual as irrelevant. But many religious people see the ritual as a strictly religious requirement, not an act rooted in the realities of life.

Sigmund Freud, who had been accused of abandoning his religion, defended himself in this way:

> And if a questioner should ask [me]: "What Judaism, if any, remains as part of you, since you have relinquished all that you have in common with your people?" [I] would answer, "Still very much, almost certainly the core and the essence."

Freud felt that his groundbreaking psychoanalytic work fulfilled the core and the essence of what Judaism was meant to be. He felt that in his daily work he was dealing with the realities of life, that is, the true purpose of the rituals and sacrifices in the first place.

With that in mind, let's take a look at the six types of sacrifices the Bible describes and relate them to the realities of our own lives to discover new ways we might talk to God, come closer to God, and offer Him something of ourselves, thus growing in our spirituality.

• *The burnt offering,* called *olah,* after the Hebrew word meaning "to go up," is the highest form of sacrifice. When we offer an *olah* to God, we are not pleased with where we are in life in relationship to Him, and we are striving to become more spiritual. We all fall sometimes. We all feel estranged from God sometimes. Through the *olah,* we express our desire to keep climbing, to keep coming closer to God.

We can make this offering through prayer in a synagogue, a church, or a meadow. We can make this offering by striving to imbue ordinary things with the divine. We can make this offering through our life's work (like Freud), through creating a spiritual atmosphere in our homes, or through music, poetry, or art.

• *The meal offering,* called *mincha,* meaning "gift to God," is brought with the frame of mind that we want to express gratitude to God for all the good things in our lives, such as food, shelter, comfort, and security.

When things are going well, it is easy to take what we have for granted. All too often, people show up at religious services when some calamity has befallen them, but rarely does a person show up simply to express gratitude.

I have often observed the same phenomenon among patients in the hospital. In most cases, only when life is threatened do they begin to appreciate its gifts. One cancer patient told me, after weeks of chemotherapy and confinement to bed, that just walking outside and feeling the sun's rays felt special. Previously, he had taken it for granted, rarely remembering to thank God for this gift.

An old Jewish tale tells of a poor farmer who had a large family that was crammed together in a small space, making life very uncomfortable. The farmer went to his rabbi for advice. The rabbi told him to take his sheep, cattle, chickens, and other animals into his home. The man and his wife complied; suddenly, there was no room for anything, and the house was filthy and noisy. The man returned to the rabbi, reporting that life was now truly impossible. The rabbi advised him to remove the animals, and the man once again complied. A short time later, the rabbi met the man on the street and asked him, "How are things?" "Wonderful," the farmer replied. "I never realized how much room we have."

• *The thanksgiving offering*, called *todah*, after the Hebrew word for "gratitude," is a thank-you to God following a narrow escape.

One day when I was riding in a car with a friend, he pulled out too far into traffic, and as he was hastily backing up to avoid being hit, an elderly female pedestrian crossed behind his car. Either he forgot to look in his rearview mirror or he missed seeing her because of a blind spot, but he almost hit her. We could both feel the electricity coursing over our nerve endings as we realized what could have happened. And we immediately said a short *todah* prayer.

All of us, especially those of us who drive to work on busy highways, have such narrow escapes almost daily. We need not think about it long to realize how easily our lives could be ruined if we were hurt or if we accidentally maimed someone else. It's my personal opinion that no one can possibly say enough *todah* prayers.

• *The peace offering* is called *shelamim,* which means "becoming whole." When we feel that different parts within us are not in sync with one another, we bring *shelamim* to God in order to achieve harmony in our life. This type of offering reflects our yearning for inner balance, inner peace. Few of us achieve it. Some of us are more perceptive and therefore perhaps more judgmental. Others of us are more sensitive to the feelings of others and therefore perhaps more compassionate. Yet we yearn to bring all those aspects of ourselves into a harmonious, well-developed, well-integrated whole. An offering of *shelamim* helps us do so.

It is never too late to develop the undeveloped parts of ourselves. Rabbi Akiva spent his childhood and young adulthood as a shepherd. He was illiterate until the age of forty, when the opportunity to begin learning Hebrew was presented to him. He wondered if it wasn't too late to learn but decided to go forward, and eventually he became one of the greatest biblical scholars who ever lived.

Anna Mary Robertson Moses spent most of her life as a farmer's wife. In her late seventies, she began to paint rural scenes for her own pleasure. Today, her works hang in museums all over the world, and there is hardly anyone who hasn't heard of Grandma Moses. It is fascinating to note that, according to the *Funk and Wagnalls Encyclopedia,* "her work is characterized by *harmonious* arrangement of figures" (emphasis mine).

• *The sin offering,* called *chatas,* comes from the Hebrew word *chet,* meaning "sin," and also "to miss." We bring a *chatas* when we have missed the mark. We shot an arrow and it landed in the wrong place, metaphorically speaking; we are sorry we didn't aim better.

A client of mine, a man in his thirties, told me how he had come to understand the meaning of sin and of *chatas*. On a hot Sunday afternoon, he had gone hiking alone in a Santa Monica canyon. He failed to pay adequate attention to the trail markers and soon found himself lost and disoriented. He sat down on a rock and calmly gathered his wits about him. During that time of rest and reflection, he had an insight. As he told me later, "Rabbi, I suddenly understood what it means to miss the mark and to go astray." Fortunately, he found his way back.

• *The guilt offering*, called *asham*, means, not surprisingly, "guilt." We might have already brought a *chatas*, but we still feel guilty. So to alleviate our guilt, we bring an *asham*.

We all feel guilt. Sometimes it is possible to make up with someone we've hurt and obtain forgiveness. But what if a person has died? Many people become estranged from their parents as a result of hurts inflicted by both sides. If a parent dies, the relationship is unresolved and the guilt preys on the survivor's mind.

The Bible understands these things. It tells us that guilt is endemic to the life that God has created. Everyone has feelings of guilt. But if we come closer to God and talk to Him about the guilt, the guilt will be lessened.

However, this path requires pure intention. The prophet Isaiah warns that offering sacrifices or prayers means nothing in the eyes of God if they are insincere. One cannot intentionally commit wrong and count on the power of prayer or an offer of sacrifice to right things with God. He quotes God: *"Why do you bring to Me the multitude of your sacrifices? . . . Though you pray at length, I will not listen, while your hands are stained with blood."*

In the modern world, this warning also applies to the motives behind philanthropy. We cannot buy a place in heaven by giving our money away on our deathbed. The intention behind our generosity is paramount. Similarly, the *attitude* with which we give is essential. Many a wealthy man gives without acknowledging that he is able to do so because God has been good to him. Were he to acknowledge this fact, he would give out of gratitude for what he himself had been given. He would give out of compassion for those who have less. Without compassion, philanthropy is just another kind of bribe.

This brings us to what sacrifice—and prayer—is not.

• Clearly, it is not a bribe. It is an offering of love.
• It is not a rote, religious observance, reserved for weekends. It is a daily conversation with God, and as such it can be scheduled or spontaneous. In the Bible, when people had the need, desire, or urge, they prayed.
• It is not a complaint. It is proper for us to pray if we are angry, but if we are still angry after we have finished praying, our prayers have somehow gone astray
• It is not a substitute for effort. If you partied all night and did not study for a test, it is blasphemy to ask God for a passing grade.
• It is not a one-way street. Prayer is not a monologue. As I mentioned in Chapter 4, prayer is a dialogue and God *does* answer us. Our job is to attune our inner ears to hear Him.
• Prayer is not socialized medicine, as the late Israeli professor Yeshayahu Leibowitz once pointed out to me. Prayer is not like walking into a clinic and getting the prescription you requested. Prayer is sharing your life with God.
• Prayer is not a guarantee. As the country-and-western ballad by Garth Brooks goes, "Sometimes God's greatest gifts are unanswered prayers." God knows best which prayers to answer.

Not long ago, a young Israeli soldier, Nachshon Waxman, was kidnapped by terrorists. His mother, Esther, ignited all of secular

Israel with her pleas for everyone's prayers. She even appeared on the *Today* show, asking mothers the world over to light candles for her son and pray for his safe return. Nevertheless, the terrorists murdered her son. Later, Nachshon's father told all those grieving, "Sometimes God says no."

Some of those moved by the Waxmans' plight were praying for the first time ever. Afterward, with great arrogance, they expressed anger that their one weak effort had not yielded instant results. We can't just go to synagogue on Yom Kippur, to a church on Easter, or to a mosque during Ramadan and start praying, then complain, "God didn't appear to me."

AS WE SAW IN THE OPENING WORDS OF THE BOOK OF LEVITICUS, God's calls come unexpectedly. Most spiritually minded people want to be ready for the call, want not to disappoint themselves or God. We never know when the burning bush might appear, but wouldn't we all want to respond as Moses did if it appeared to us?

If you play basketball, God may one day appear to you on the basketball court, but recognizing God and responding appropriately take some preparation. In other words, you have to nurture your relationship with God if you hope to be able to recognize Him. This process requires a lot of training and preparation, as well as the right attitude. How do we acquire the right attitude?

This chapter has offered an approach to that question. I hope that it has also contributed to our understanding of the purposes of prayer, which are to help us become more spiritual by asking God to remember us well and to work out issues, problems, and challenges within ourselves so that our lives can be more harmonious. Prayer represents the ability to say "thank you"; to recognize that we have sinned and will sin and that this is part of life; and to recognize that, as guilt is endemic to humanity, we must try to work it through as best as we know how.

If we take this approach to prayer, we may also gain a better understanding of what religion is. Religion was not meant to be confined to a synagogue, church, or mosque but rather to address all aspects of life. Religion deals with all of life from the viewpoint of the soul, as we shall continue to see.

19

Intention

WE HAVE JUST FINISHED A DISCUSSION OF ATTITUDE.
And what goes with attitude more than intention? This issue of
intention brings us to one of the more dramatic, though possibly
less well known, stories of the Bible.

The Israelites have erected the sanctuary, and now they are
ready to make their first sacrifice. They have been well prepared for
this task by their leader, Moses, and by Moses's brother, Aaron, the
high priest.

It is not surprising that the first sacrifice is a sin offering and
that it is a calf that is slaughtered and burnt. This offering is
clearly being made to atone for the collective sin of the Israelites
in worshiping the golden calf. Other sacrifices are also offered, and
then *"the Presence of the Lord appeared to all the people. Fire came forth
from before the Lord and consumed the burnt offering and the fat parts on
the altar. And all the people saw, and shouted, and fell on their faces."*

There is great jubilation. The first sacrifice has been accepted.

Everything has gone well, and everyone is happy. They fall onto their faces as an expression of thanksgiving and gratitude, and they feel a real connection with God, who has accepted their offering joyfully. Then something terrible happens.

The sons of Aaron, Nadab and Abihu, who have assisted their father in his priestly duties, decide to put incense into the sacrificial vessels, thus presenting an offering God did not request. The Bible tells us that a strange fire ignites, and it is so fierce that it consumes Nadab and Abihu on the spot.

What's going on here? Why does God react in such an angry way to this unbidden sacrifice? Is this not an act of *olah,* voluntary gift giving? Hardly.

Remember that God knows with what intentions Nadab and Abihu are making their offering. He is apparently so offended by their intentions that He rejects the offering with great vehemence, causing the fire not to ascend toward heaven but to turn on Nadab and Abihu instead. God knew that the brothers were showing off. These two young men were not satisfied with assisting their father, the high priest; they were already wondering when their own turn to assume leadership would come.

This is a common problem among the very young, which Freud named "Thanatos," after the Greek word for "death." In Freudian psychology, Thanatos represents the unconscious wish for the death of an authority figure. A younger person erroneously thinks that he cannot come into his own so long as an older person lives. As long as that elder is present, the younger person feels like a child and often behaves like one.

The children of prominent people experience this problem perhaps more acutely than others. Malcolm Forbes documented this phenomenon quite convincingly in his book *What Happened to Their Kids: Children of the Rich and Famous.* In it he quotes Randolph Churchill, the son of Winston Churchill: "When you are living under the shadow of a great oak tree, the small sapling, so close to the parent tree, does not perhaps receive enough sunshine."

This was apparently how Nadab and Abihu felt. They wanted the limelight, but God would not permit them to grab it under the guise of serving the Lord; hence the vehemence of the punishment.

The story of God's rejection of Nadab and Abihu's sacrifice has rather startling similarities to the story of Cain and Abel and the first act of sacrifice recounted in the Bible.

Cain and Abel each bring a sacrifice to God. Abel, the shepherd, brings the best of his flock. Cain, the farmer, brings some *"fruit of the earth,"* and you get the idea that it is not the choicest produce. God accepts Abel's sacrifice but rejects Cain's. (Then, of course, Cain kills Abel out of jealousy and subsequently declares, *"Am I my brother's keeper?"*) The point of the story is that intention counts. God cares about the frame of mind with which one offers a sacrifice.

Consider what it meant for Abel, a poor shepherd, to bring the best ram of his flock to be offered to God. Not only did he deny himself and his family a potential meal, he also denied his flock the offspring the ram might have sired. It was an act of pure love. In today's world, such an act could be compared to that of an architect who designs the house of his dreams and then burns the plans on the altar, giving his best work to God. Or it could be compared to a writer who finishes the great American novel but, instead of sending it off to a publisher, offers it to God alone. Meanwhile, Cain offers something he can spare—some average fruit.

So intention is clearly paramount.

Some religious people might argue that God considers action most important or that God considers faith most important. However, I submit that the Bible is showing us dramatically, and repeatedly, that the thought and intention behind an action are just as important as the act itself, if not more so.

Right after the world is created and the very first sacrifice is offered, one form of sacrifice is accepted while another is rejected, and fratricide and death come into existence. The Ten Commandments stress the importance of thought, so much so that the commandments relating to thought—the first and the tenth—begin and end the recitation of prescriptions and prohibitions relating to words and behavior. When the sanctuary is completed, God again accepts one form of sacrifice but rejects another, and again death comes into the world. If the punishment seems severe, it is because God is trying to drive this message home.

But, you might argue, we don't bring sacrifices today. So why should we care about Cain and Abel or Nadab and Abihu?

Consider the lesson in Chapter 14: God doesn't care only about how we act toward Him; He cares how we act toward one another *and with what intentions we relate to one another.* Truth be told, we also care about that. At one time or another, each of us has probably been disappointed by a fine gift because we sensed that the motives of the gift giver were questionable. Perhaps the gift came from a friend whose gift giving was likely to have strings attached. Perhaps it came from a business associate who was likely to demand a favor or follow up the gift with a sales pitch. Perhaps it came from a loved one and implied a guilty conscience. If we have had such suspicions, it means we mistrusted the intention behind the gift giving.

As a rule, children have even finer antennae than adults for this sort of thing. One divorced father told me how hurt he was when his eight-year-old son refused to play with a new, expensive computer he had bought for the boy's birthday. After some self-examination, the father realized that with his extravagant gift he had been trying to assuage his guilt at missing several visits with his son. Sensing this, the boy refused to be bought off, and he let his father know of his hurt feelings in no uncertain terms.

Giving gifts with strings attached can scar children who may be too shy to express their feelings as this boy did. A friend told me how, as a child, she had been presented with a violin by her father.

"I remember it so well—my father sat me up on the kitchen table so he could talk to me eye to eye. He told me in very serious tones that his father, who had been an accomplished musician, had offered to teach him to play, but he had refused and regretted it ever since. He said he hoped that I wouldn't make the same mistake. He then gave me this little violin and told me that it had cost a great deal of money, but that there was still time to take it back. 'Do you want me to take it back?' he asked sternly. 'No,' I said, feeling the weight of the world on my shoulders. I hated that violin with a passion. It was a poorly made child's violin which sounded more like a hungry cat than a musical instrument. My father couldn't find a small enough case for it, so he had bought a regular, large case, and this little violin rattled in it as I dragged it along the ground on my way to the hated music lessons."

She told the story in an amusing way, but it is a sad story of a child who was not given a gift at all. She was asked to carry a burden of guilt for an adult who could not forgive himself for his own childhood mistake. He should have been glad his own father had given him a choice and that he had had the freedom to say no, something he did not give his daughter.

Gift giving isn't the only act in which intentions are paramount. Actually, there is no human interaction in which intention does *not* count. In a close relationship, our partner always senses the intentions behind our actions. Intention counts in intimacy, in sensuality, and in sex. Intention counts in love. Intention counts in charity.

Maimonides, the great medieval physician and philosopher, teaches that the highest level of charity is getting someone a job, and in such a way that he doesn't know you got it for him. This is because, in so doing, you have given this man a gift of the greatest value—you have restored his dignity, and you have not created a debt of gratitude.

When a man's dignity is restored, his self-esteem and sense of well-being are restored. If he feels good about himself, he can go out and conquer the world. If he feels lousy about himself, he doesn't have the strength to pick up a pencil. Restoring someone's dignity is truly a gift of pure intention. The gift giver gains only the secret joy of knowing a good deed has been done.

Of course, this brings up the question of how we form the right intention. Being basically selfish human beings, how do we purge ourselves of our less-than-altruistic motives and do things right?

I haven't any secret formulas to offer, but I have come across two bits of wonderful advice from two very disparate sources. The key is *to see clearly and hear well.* If that seems cryptic, allow me to elaborate.

Viktor Frankl said this about seeing clearly: When we have good eyesight, we see only out. When we have a cataract, we actually see part of our own eye. So the scope of our vision is limited, and we focus in the wrong direction. It is easier to formulate a pure intention when one is able to transcend oneself—to see out rather than narcissistically focusing only on oneself.

D. H. Lawrence described hearing well as "listening to the whispers of the wall."

What do most of us do when we walk into a house? We start to talk. But we should listen. To whom? To the people already there and to the atmosphere of the place. This is the same advice God gave Moses when He told him to take off his shoes. Be sensitive to what is beneath your feet, God said. To that we might add, be sensitive to what is in front of your eyes and what your ears pick up. If you invest energy in being sensitive to the things that surround you, you will not be preoccupied with your own concerns. Then your intentions will be able to flow from a higher place and ascend toward heaven.

20

Sex

LET'S BE CLEAR ABOUT ONE THING: THE BIBLE IS NOT prudish. There's a lot of sex in the Bible, which presents the sexual nature of humanity as one of God's gifts to be enjoyed. On the other hand, the Bible recognizes the animalistic side of this powerful drive, as we discussed in Chapter 16, so it gives us some definite guidelines on how to enjoy and when. In Leviticus we find some of those guidelines, which, to a modern reader, may seem quite strange.

For example, the text states, *"If a man has sexual relations with a woman, they shall bathe in water and remain* tamey *until evening."* Many scholars have puzzled over that word *tamey,* and to this day no one truly knows the meaning of it. Since the word is used repeatedly to connote a withdrawal from appearing in public and is seen often in conjunction with prescriptions for ritual baths, it has typically been translated as "unclean." However, I submit that the word neither means nor implies anything of the sort. If one looks closely at the context of the passage, it becomes clear that it simply means "private." So the sentence actually reads, *"If a man has sexual relations with a woman, they shall bathe in water and remain private until evening."*

So what should they be doing together until evening? Being together.

This is the biblical teaching of how to develop a deeper level of intimacy, what might be called "afterplay." The Bible is saying that the sexual experience is so important that both individuals should take time out afterward just to be together. They can talk with each other and get to know each other on the new level to which the intimacy of sex has brought them.

Note that often when the Bible speaks of people having sex, it uses the verb "to know," as in *"Now Adam knew his wife, Eve, and she conceived and bore Cain."*

This is meant to be taken literally. Sex should be a way in which one person gets to know another, in which both parties discover each other's weaknesses and vulnerabilities, each other's strengths and hidden talents. How important is this? It is the very secret of a stable, happy marriage.

In a recent newspaper column, Dr. Joyce Brothers summed up the latest research on marital infidelity. It is a myth, she points out, that most acts of infidelity occur simply because someone attractive comes along. "Infidelity is more apt to result when something is missing within the primary relationship, such as lack of communication. The inability to share experiences and disappointments often leads to resentment or boredom."

One of my clients, a married woman, entered into a passionate extramarital affair, subsequently deciding to divorce her nice but boring husband. Her lover was likewise tired of his nagging wife and the dreary routine of his marriage. After they were both "free," the lovers married. But clearly, their ways of communicating had not undergone any change, because soon enough she began to

think her second husband was kind of boring, too, and he started
to complain that she was becoming a dreary nag.

In therapy, as we examined what had gone wrong, it became
clear that there had been very little true communication in either
the first or the second marriage, whether verbal or sexual. These
people had merely been masturbating, using each other for that
purpose. The so-called passionate sex had led to exhaustion and
sleep, not to a greater level of intimacy or spirituality.

Psychologists have a saying, "Orgasm takes place not between
the legs but between the ears." The French put it another way: "It's
not the sex, it's the cigarette afterward." They both mean, of course,
that the intimate conversation—the depth of self-revelation inspired by sex—is of greater value than the physical release. Of
course, the Bible sees sex not simply as a physical release but as an
awe-inspiring experience.

In sex, we experience a temporary oneness with each other and
with the universe. We perceive our connection to a world without
end, to a sense of omnipotence and immortality.

This notion is not the Bible's alone. We find it in many cultures
and traditions. In Hindi, it is *atman,* meaning "total unity with
the world at large." In Latin, it is *amor,* possibly a combination of
a, meaning "without," and *mors,* meaning "death," thus equating
love with immortality.

So we recognize that sex is a monumental experience. And the
Bible is saying that it is such a monumental experience that it
should be inconceivable to get up the next morning as if nothing
had ever happened and rush off to a medical appointment or to the
office or to an aerobics class.

Yet that is exactly what many of us do. We jump out of bed and
plunge back into our hectic, fast-paced world. Some of my clients
have told me that for them sex is much better when they are on vacation. They can be more relaxed, open, and free to bond when
they know that the next day they can lounge in bed without having to rush off anywhere. During the rest of the year, there is never

any time specifically penciled in on their busy calendars for special moments of togetherness and true emotional intimacy.

So should we have sex only on vacation? Obviously not, but perhaps, just as we take sick leave, we should take "love leave" from time to time as well. This is really what that cryptic biblical passage is all about: It is a prescription to take "love leave."

There's more.

Shortly after that comes another passage that might appear equally mystifying to the modern reader: *"And if a woman has a discharge, her discharge being blood from her body, she shall be in a state known as* temayah *for seven days."*

So here again we see that word, but now in its feminine form, and again it means not "unclean" but "private." The Bible is clearly saying that the woman is to be afforded privacy during her menstruation, that she is entitled to "menstrual leave."

Another radical idea for the modern world? Let's examine it carefully and see just how in tune with the times it might be.

In ancient societies, women were given time off to reconstitute their energies during menstruation. This was crucial for their functioning in society. Here is what Clarissa Pinkola Estés writes in *Women Who Run with the Wolves:*

> In order to converse with the wild feminine, a woman must temporarily leave the world and inhabit a state of aloneness in the oldest sense of the word. Long ago the word *alone* was treated as two words, *all one.* To be *all one* meant to be wholly one. . . . That is precisely the goal of solitude, to be all one. . . . Women from ancient times as well as modern aboriginal women set a sacred place aside for this communion and inquiry. Traditionally it is said to have been set aside during women's menses, for during that time a woman lives much closer to self-knowing than usual. . . . Feelings, memories, sensations that are normally blocked from consciousness pass over into cognizance without resistance.

So we see that throughout history and in many different societies, this private time was considered very important. Every woman needs "a room of one's own," to borrow the words of Virginia Woolf. Yet throughout the generations, women have often been denied this.

I had to deal with this very issue recently, when a male client came into my office. The first words out of his mouth were "I hope this doesn't shock you, but I'm married to two women at the same time." Before I had time to react, he told me not to take his statement literally. He went on to explain how his wife's hormonal swings affected her moods and their relationship. They had discussed this problem, and the wife had acknowledged that he was right. Medications prescribed by her doctor had been of some help but had not solved the problem.

As this couple owned a weekend home, I suggested they spend perhaps one weekend a month apart in order to give the wife some time of her own to reconstitute herself. It proved to be precisely what was needed, and a much better solution than drugs.

Of course, this was an extreme solution. Most people don't own weekend homes; most don't even have an extra room in the house to set aside. But it is possible, if both partners make a conscious effort to do so, to give the wife some *emotional space* once a month. This could be a time when the husband takes a greater role in child care and domestic duties. If the wife usually fixes the meals, perhaps he could cook or take the family out to dinner. Small gestures can go a long way toward making the other person—whose body is undergoing dramatic hormonal changes and a significant loss of blood accompanied by a loss of iron, calcium, and other minerals—feel nurtured.

Is more of a burden, then, being placed on the man? Not at all. He is using this time to develop more sensitivity and tenderness. In so doing, he is developing his feminine side, which is essential if he, too, is to become a whole human being. Meanwhile, his wife, who is more free to perceive herself as a separate individual, distinct from her husband, is now free to develop her masculine qualities of independence.

At this time, the Bible further instructs the husband, *"Do not come near a woman during her period of privacy to uncover her nakedness."* In other words, sex is off limits.

Is this an old-fashioned, prudish idea steeped in superstition or another secret of a happy marriage? By now, you can probably predict my response.

So many people come to me complaining that desire has left their marriage, that spontaneity is gone, that sex has become progressively more rote and less frequent. They miss the time when they were first married and they felt passion and excitement. I have discovered that, more often than not, these couples are not really complaining about sexual incompatibility; what they miss is emotional intimacy.

Scratch the surface, and you find an unfulfilled desire for nurturing and respect. Nurturing conveys the message that you can be loved for who you are, with all your foibles, frailties, and vulnerabilities. To respect means to reinspect, to take another look, to see the other person as he or she really is, and to accept that person.

This is why the first part of the Bible's admonition, which we covered in the opening of this chapter, is so important. When you come together in the intimacy of sex, take the time to be together, to get to know each other. As you get to know each other better, you will become more sensitive to each other's needs, and your respect for each other will grow. During the time of the woman's menses, take time to be emotionally apart.

"Let there be spaces in your togetherness," the poet Kahlil Gibran wrote in 1923. His words couldn't be truer today; both partners need that space. Having been apart, you will come together with fresh excitement. We all know that when something is denied us, we crave it all the more. If we diet, denying ourselves strawberry shortcake until we get to a certain weight, how delicious it seems when we have reached our goal and can allow ourselves to indulge again!

When a husband and wife are committed to being apart—for the good and greater growth of each—their reunion will be all that much sweeter. Such is age-old wisdom, and such is the advice of the Bible.

21

Love

IN THE LANGUAGE OF TODAY'S WORLD, IN WHICH THE WORD "love" has become commonplace, in which we love ice cream and love going to the movies and love our new computers or new clothes, it is hard to convey what the Bible means when it says "love." Writer-producer George Englund has said that the word "love" is now so meaningless that "it ought to be taken out behind the woodshed and shot."

But in the absence of a better substitute, we will struggle with the word, attempting to infuse it with the meaning it had 3,200 years ago. When the Bible was written, the word "love" was sacred. Among the thousands of words that appear in the Five Books of Moses, the word "love" appears in only four commandments. *Only four!*

We see it twice in the Book of Leviticus and twice more in the Book of Deuteronomy. Each phrase that contains the word "love" is short and to the point, conveying a commandment from God, telling us whom and how we should love. Interestingly enough, the love the Bible speaks of is not romantic love between man and woman, nor is it the love between parent and child. (Indeed, we are commanded to "honor" our parents, not necessarily to love them.)

The Bible speaks of a completely different kind of love, an extraordinary kind of love, the kind of love that can move mountains, heal the world, and unite all humankind:

"You shall love your neighbor as yourself."

"You shall love the stranger as yourself."

"You shall love the Lord your God."

"You shall love the stranger, for you were strangers in the land of Egypt."

These commandments, particularly the commandment to love your neighbor, are found in the teachings of all the world's religions. Indeed, the idea has been adopted by nearly every religion and ethical belief system in the world in its practical form, better known today as the Golden Rule. As far back as 600 B.C.E., we find this in the *Analects* of Confucius: "What you do not yourself desire, do not put before others." We also find it in the teachings of Hillel from the first century B.C.E.: "What is hurtful to yourself do not do to your fellowman. . . . That is the whole of the Torah and the rest is but commentary." And we find similar statements in the writings of Plato, Aristotle, Socrates, and Seneca.

Buddhism teaches, "Hurt not others with that which pains yourself."

Christianity teaches, "In everything, do to others what you would have them do to you."

Hinduism teaches, "Treat others as you would yourself be treated. Do nothing to your neighbor that hereafter you would not have your neighbor do to you."

Islam teaches, "Do unto all men as you would wish to have done unto you; reject for others what you would reject for yourselves."

Zoroastrianism teaches, "That nature alone is good which refrains from doing unto another whatsoever is not good for itself."

But note that while it is admirable to treat your neighbor as yourself and not do him harm, the 3,200-year-old biblical prescription goes much farther than that. *"You shall love your neighbor as yourself,"* it commands.

Additionally, the thing a lot of people seem to forget when quoting these immortal words is that the sentence does not stop there. It actually says, *"Love your neighbor as yourself; I am the Lord."* That is because loving your neighbor as yourself is impossible if you do not link that concept to God.

There is another catch. In Hebrew, right before the word for "neighbor," is the preposition *le,* which most translators simply ignore. But that little word *le* means that you must love *all* of your neighbor; and you must love your neighbor not just in theory but in practice.

A tall assignment? To be sure. Which is why God must be in the equation.

It is possible to obey this awesome commandment—to love another person completely—only if you can first completely love yourself. To do that, you must first acknowledge and respect the divine image that resides in yourself. Then you will be able to see it in every other human being.

To put it another way, the first order of business is that you be able to love and accept yourself; only then can you love your neighbor as yourself; only then can you have a basis for comparison.

Before there is any misunderstanding, let me lay one myth to rest once and for all. Selfishness is not, by any stretch of the imagination, love of self. Selfishness is a preoccupation with the self by a person who is not able to love himself or herself.

Erich Fromm, in *The Art of Loving,* teaches us, "Selfishness and self-love, far from being identical, are actually opposites. The selfish person does not love himself too much but too little; in fact he hates himself." Don't think of loving yourself as being selfish; think of it as a commandment.

How do you love yourself? You must recognize all the good things and all the bad things that are part of you: your abusive mother, your chronic illness, your bad first marriage, your exceptional memory, your love of nature, your love of children, your perfectionism, your artistic abilities—in other words, everything, whether bad or good, that makes you who you are. You must recognize these things. You must embrace them. You must accept who you are. You must respect yourself. Only then can you embrace, accept, and respect your neighbor in the same way.

When you adopt such a mind-set, all the things you do to make yourself better and nurture yourself—things like enjoying art or music, writing, walking, dancing, studying the Bible, appreciating nature, traveling, praying—can become infused with a new and special purpose.

It's also important to like being with yourself. It's good to have friends, of course, but first of all you must like having yourself for company. If you don't, who will?

Oriah Mountain Dreamer, a contemporary shaman, wrote a poem on this subject. She concludes it with these words: "I want to know if you can be alone with yourself, and if you truly like the company you keep in the empty moments." Can you answer "yes"? The deeper you go in examining your own strengths and weaknesses—your bright side and your shadow side—the more accepting and forgiving you can become of the same traits in others.

One physician, a cardiologist, told me he had always felt he was a very capable doctor, but he had not realized how unaware he really was of his own weaknesses and vulnerabilities. In fact, he had arrogantly believed that his medical knowledge set him apart from the fears and insecurities he observed in his patients. Only when he underwent coronary bypass surgery did he realize how wrong he had been. For the first time, he had to experience the discomfort and indignity of being hospitalized, controlled by others, helpless. Only then did he truly connect with his patients and begin to understand what *"love your neighbor as yourself"* really implies.

"LOVE THE STRANGER" COULD BE SEEN AS JUST ANOTHER WAY OF saying "love your neighbor," but the word "stranger" seems to imply that we must love even the person we know least of all.

The importance of being kind to the stranger was introduced in the Book of Exodus. When the Israelites first escaped from Egypt, they were told to understand the feelings of the stranger, because they, too, had been strangers in a strange land. In other words, they were told to identify their experiences with the experiences of the stranger. Thus they would be able to understand the pain and suffering of others.

In the Book of Leviticus, perhaps because the connection between self-understanding and the understanding of another has been made, God commands, *"love the stranger."* The secret is that the stranger is not really someone else. The stranger is all of us. And that is really the point of all of these commandments that tell us to love: Acknowledge God within yourself, and in so doing you will see and love God in your fellow human beings.

Shakespeare gave us his version of this commandment in *Hamlet:* "This above all—to thine own self be true, and it must follow, as the night the day, thou canst not then be false to any man." Note that the admonition to be true to yourself has one purpose only—that you cannot then be false to another person.

Fascinating idea, this: that our eternal quest to face ourselves, accept ourselves, improve ourselves, to see in ourselves the image of God, to reflect the divine element on earth, is there just so that, ultimately, we can love someone else.

22

Loving Truth, Loving Lies

IN THIS CHAPTER, WE TAKE A LOOK AT ANOTHER KEY COMponent of love: truth. Specifically, we examine when, in the course of loving our fellow human beings, it is essential to tell the truth and when it is essential to lie.

You read that right. The Bible tells us that sometimes lying is not only permissible, but actually *mandated.*

Surprised? The Bible is full of surprises. But before we examine the tricky issue of justifiable lies, let's give truth its due.

There is no question that the Bible holds honesty in very high regard. In the Book of Genesis, we saw God's displeasure at the lies told by Adam and Eve and His wrath at the lies of Cain. In Exodus, we saw lying expressly forbidden in two of the Ten Commandments—*"You shall not swear falsely by the name of the Lord your God"* and *"You shall not bear false witness against your neighbor"*—and reiterated again: *"Keep far from falsehood; do not bring death on those who are innocent and in the right."*

In Leviticus, the Bible discusses another kind of honesty: honesty in business and personal dealings between people. On this subject, several commandments are given, in particular, these two: *"You shall not deal deceitfully or falsely with one another"* and *"Do not wrong one another, but fear your God; for I the Lord am your God."*

Clearly, the Bible is interested in fair and honest business practices. This might mean that if, for instance, you are a grocery store owner and an earthquake has damaged other nearby stores, you cannot take advantage of your customers by charging unfairly high prices just because they have nowhere else to go.

Furthermore, the Bible is interested in preventing the kinds of wrongs that can be committed through the misuse of words. For example, imagine you know that your neighbor has a dark past. Let us say that, some years ago, he was involved with drugs and alcohol and perhaps even has a criminal record. In order to deal with that person fairly, you may not mention any of that to him. Even though speaking of those things would mean you were being truthful, it still would not be fair—and therefore would be wrong, according to the Bible. Fascinating, isn't it?

Also considered a violation is another kind of truth, the truth of blame. This is a dilemma I come across in the hospital all the time. Someone who is obese and smokes four packs of cigarettes a day comes in with congestive heart failure. According to the Bible, you are not allowed to say to him or her, "Look at you! You brought this disease on yourself, and now your loved ones have to suffer." While such a statement would be true, it would be cruel to blame this person now, when he or she is experiencing fear and suffering. It would be cruel, it would be unfair, and it would be wrong.

You also cannot say to this person, "You led a terribly wasteful life, and now God is punishing you for it." This is not for you to judge. You cannot read God's mind. Your function, in following the commandment to *"love your neighbor,"* is to be a catalyst for health and recovery.

Another category of wronging someone through words, according to the Bible, is to give wrong advice. This one is a minefield. If you have friends, you are undoubtedly taken into their confidence, and in response you consciously or unconsciously give advice. How are you to know what is right or wrong advice?

The answer is that the advice you give must be tailor-made to that person. It cannot be advice that, were your friend to follow it, would benefit you in some way. You may not tell this person what you think he or she wants to hear or withhold what you know that person needs to hear, just to preserve the friendship. And when you give advice that might be painful to hear, you must be gentle; cruelty masquerading as truth is always wrong.

Giving advice to anyone while staying within these boundaries is very difficult. It takes a lot of thought and care. Taking that kind of thought, care, time, and energy to help someone is what it truly means to obey the commandment to *"love your neighbor."* Only if we are truthful with ourselves can we speak truthfully with our friends in the loving manner that the Bible requires. If you are truthful with yourself, you will be able to know the truth for other people as well. If you truthfully struggle to examine your needs and vulnerabilities, your strengths and weaknesses, your light and dark sides, you will also understand all these things with regard to others.

REMEMBER THAT THE BIBLE SAYS, *"DO NOT WRONG ONE ANOTHER, BUT fear your God."* The stress on fearing God is not accidental, because in certain ways fearing God helps keep us honest. We might get away with fooling someone else, but we cannot fool God.

God knows the secrets of every heart. God knows when you are trying to mislead someone, even if that person perceives your words as good advice. You may go through life seemingly saying all the right things, but on a much deeper level God knows whether your motivation is egocentric and narcissistic or altruistic and sincere.

Clearly, what can make truth a wrong and lying a right is the motivation or intention behind what is said. This applies also to what is *not* said, because acts of omission are often equal to acts of commission. "Forgetting" to call your mother on Mother's Day, when you know the hurt this will cause, is just as bad as saying something openly cruel. Likewise, according to the Bible, failing to speak out in the face of an injustice is plainly wrong.

All of us would agree that a person who fails to report a piece of information that might exonerate someone accused of a crime is committing a grave wrong. But how many of us look the other way in a work setting when one employee is wrongly blamed for the errors of another? How many of us would say in that situation, "I'd rather not get involved. . . . You know, I don't want to say anything, because I'm basically a very shy, reticent person, and it's none of my business anyway."

Not saying something goes against the commandment that tells us, *"Do not wrong one another."* You have wronged a person, even if you did not do so yourself, because you could have prevented the wrong by speaking out. Your motivation was selfish. You did not want to cause yourself any trouble, so you allowed someone else to suffer an injustice. Again, motivation is the key.

It is also motivation that sometimes requires us to lie. This is what we have come to call "the little white lie," the lie told with the best of intentions for the sake of preserving peace. We see it in the Bible on several occasions, but the two most noteworthy examples occur in the Book of Genesis.

Abraham's wife, Sarah, upon hearing that at age ninety, after having been barren her entire life, she will have a son, scoffs at the idea, remarking to herself, *"Now that I am withered, am I to have enjoyment—with my husband so old?"* Subsequently, God has a conversation with Abraham about Sarah's attitude. He reports to Abraham that Sarah said, *"Shall I in truth bear a child, old as I am?"*

From the previous sentence we know that this is not precisely what Sarah said, but *God* tells a "little white lie," omitting what might have hurt Abraham's feelings or made him angry with his wife.

The second famous incident involves the lie told by Joseph's brothers after the death of their father, Jacob. The brothers are concerned that Joseph's earlier forgiveness was motivated by his love for their father. Now that their father is dead, the brothers are afraid that their relationship might deteriorate, so they send Joseph a message that is a lie. The message reads, *"Before his death, your father left this instruction: So shall you say to Joseph, 'Forgive, I urge you, the offense and guilt of your brothers who treated you so harshly.' Therefore, please forgive the offense of the servants of the God of your father."*

Of course, Joseph, who was at his father's deathbed, knows that this is a lie. But he does not challenge it. Weeping, he only reiterates his earlier statement that in their evil deed, the brothers had, in fact, fulfilled a greater divine plan.

Is the Bible condoning this lie? Absolutely. What we learn here is that it is permissible, even desirable, to create a "healing fiction" for the sake of family peace. So if your intentions are pure, creating a healing fiction is simply another expression of love.

It won't surprise you that, throughout the centuries, various Bible commentators have engaged in long debates on this issue. One of the most famous, related in the Talmud, took place in the first century C.E. between the School of Shammai and the School of Hillel concerning how one should describe a bride on her wedding day.

The School of Shammai argued that, since the Bible clearly stated, *"keep far from falsehood,"* a bride should be described exactly as she is. In other words, if she is unattractive or clumsy, she cannot be described as beautiful and graceful. The School of Hillel, on the other hand, argued that a truth that inflicts hurt does not bring about the peace the Bible teaches, so the bride should always be described as beautiful.

The School of Hillel won the day.

Having officiated at many weddings, I can testify that just about every bride glows with happiness. If you look at her and think that she is not beautiful, the lie is within yourself. That is to say, if you are so cynical and your view of life is so skewed that you cannot see the pure happiness of another person, you might as well "lie"—because you will, ironically, be speaking the truth.

PART IV

23

Blessing

W ITH THIS CHAPTER, WE BEGIN OUR EXAMINATION OF the Fourth Book of Moses, the Book of Numbers. By the end of the first three books, most of the commandments have been given. The Israelites' task now is to get to the Promised Land. That trip, which should take only eleven days, ends up taking forty years.

Why that happens, and what we have to learn from it, is chiefly contained in the dramatic stories of the Book of Numbers, so named after a census of the Israelites that takes place early in the narrative. This is where we learn that 603,550 men, each with his household, are counted. This means that the nation of Israel probably numbers, conservatively speaking, about 3 million people. Imagine moving the inhabitants of the city of Los Angeles across California and settling them in, say, Nevada, and you have an idea of the scope of this undertaking. Yet here they all are, arranged in orderly groups around the tent that contains the Ark of the Covenant, ready to embark on the journey to the Promised Land.

The Promised Land must be understood in two ways. Of course, it is the land that was promised by God to the descendants of Abraham. But it is also a metaphysical land, the place inside ourselves that is the focus of our goals and aspirations. And we all know from the struggles of our own lives that it is not easy getting there.

The Bible tells us that, in order to get to the Promised Land, we need to have something that is both essential and intangible: a blessing.

If you don't believe a blessing is essential, consider what happens to people who do not receive the blessing of their parents, spouses, or other loved ones when they embark on a journey of transition. Are they not forever scarred by that experience? Is their new venture not markedly affected by the burden of coping with the fact that a figure of importance in their lives has withheld support?

This often happens when children choose an occupation of which their parents disapprove. Sometimes this lack of approval creates an obsessive need to excel, which can unleash a chain reaction that causes various kinds of damage.

I know of a woman, now in her forties, who comes from a long line of lawyers. She was a brilliant student, and everyone in the family expected she would pursue the traditional family profession. But she also had an aptitude for music and yearned to be a concert pianist. Her family tried hard to discourage her from this career choice, and when she won a scholarship to Juilliard, they almost broke their ties with her. She nevertheless achieved renown as a pianist and even recorded several albums. But at age thirty, she could no longer tolerate the lack of family blessing. She abruptly ended her musical career and enrolled in law school. Today, she is a successful attorney, and her parents are very proud of her; yet something inside her has been destroyed. She never plays the piano. Just how deeply scarred she is by this experience was related to me by a friend who, meaning well, surprised her by playing one of her own recordings. Her reaction was a deep depression lasting several months.

I know of another person, a man in his forties, whose father, a doctor, told him what he should do with his life while he was still a high school student. While the father didn't necessarily expect him to follow in his footsteps, he did expect his son to take up a profession of which he approved: medicine, law, or business. When the son chose a career as a documentary filmmaker, the father voiced his disappointment in the strongest terms. The son responded by becoming a workaholic, neglecting his own family just to prove to his father that he could be as financially successful as he might have been had he taken up an "approved" career. He achieved his goal. He even succeeded in impressing his father by hiring one of his father's colleagues to appear in a medical documentary he produced. But the price proved to be too high—his marriage ended in divorce.

So a blessing is very, very important.

The blessing that God commands Aaron and his sons, the priests, to confer on the people is this:

"May God bless you and protect you.

"May God make His face to shine upon you and be gracious to you.

"May God bestow His favor upon you and grant you peace!"

This blessing, particularly the first line, is famous. It is probably the most familiar blessing in the Bible. Jewish people know it, Protestant people know it, and Catholic people know it. It is so well known because it expresses one of the essentials of life.

I am reminded of the musical rendition of this blessing in the Broadway musical *Fiddler on the Roof,* because the songwriter captured the deep meaning of this blessing in his lyrics:

> May the Lord protect and defend you,
> May He always shield you from shame,
> May you come to be
> In Paradise a shining name.

If you have been blessed by God, how should you demonstrate that to the world? The answer is that you should be a shining example to others.

This idea relates directly to the very first lesson of the Bible, one to which we have returned time and again: our obligation to create divine light. We defined this divine light as energy, or the creative life force for good in the world. This blessing from the Book of Numbers is asking that we become energized by the light of God, so that we can do the creative work expected of us.

Yet, thus blessed, we must still remain humble. Why? It is no accident that the Hebrew word for "blessing," *bracha,* is rooted in the word *berech,* meaning "bended knees," a symbol of humility. In other words, if you have been blessed by God, if God's light has shone upon you, if God has been gracious to you, that blessing should be there for everyone to see. It should shine in your face, your character, your demeanor, and the sense of humility about yourself that you impart to others.

We all have met people whom we might admiringly describe as "gracious." We mean, of course, that these people are kind and obliging, willing to extend themselves to others. To act this way is to be imbued with God's grace, God's blessing.

THIS BRINGS US TO THE KEY DIFFERENCE BETWEEN COGNITION AND experience, between knowing something and living it. You could enroll in a seminary and study religion for years, yet not be religious. This is because religion, even if we seem to have forgotten it, is synonymous with the way we live. Study is important, but study is meaningless if it is not put to use. We might know all the biblical citations and have read tomes by philosophers and theologians on the subject of loving one's neighbor, but the bottom line is what we *do.* Do we exude positive energy by being kind and helpful, or are we a negative force, constantly difficult or critical?

I strongly recommend the book *An Interrupted Life: The Diaries of Etty Hillesum, 1941–43.* Etty, by all accounts, was a person who shone with grace and love, and her testament lives on long after she is gone. Even on her way to Auschwitz, knowing that death surely awaited her, she considered her life a blessing. That is because she knew what it is to "be a blessing."

If you have been blessed, act in such a way that you *become* that blessing. Indeed, according to the Bible, this is a "categorical imperative," to borrow Immanuel Kant's phrase. If you can take "be a blessing" as your categorical imperative, as the unconditional command of your conscience—which means that you follow this guideline in all that you do—you will be a blessing to yourself, your family, your community, and all of humanity.

How do you live this ideal, practically speaking? Well, at least you should look presentable. At least you should smile. You should be the type of person who makes others feel better when you walk into a room. In the hospital where I work, it is easy to see who meets this standard. Exhausted by pain, patients sense instantly whether a person walking into the room brings warmth and peace or disquiet and toxicity, be that person a nurse, doctor, friend, or relative. I think this is why Jews greet each other with the phrase *Shalom aleichem* and Muslims say *Salaam aleikhem* ("Peace be with you"). Implied in this greeting is the hope that the visitor does indeed bring a spirit of peace. To the extent that you can walk into any room and bring peace with you—as the blessing from the Book of Numbers says—you can advance toward the Promised Land.

Furthermore, you will find that being blessed means being surrounded by people who will help you. It will be as if you have become a magnet for all the good that is near you. And God will help, too.

On this subject, W. H. Murray wrote, "The moment one definitely commits oneself, then Providence moves, too. All sorts of things occur to help one that would never have occurred."

So you can count on all sorts of help. No one can get to the Promised Land under his or her own power. But you have to start on your own. Once you do begin—watch what happens!

Tradition tells us that when the Israelites first escaped from Egypt and reached the Sea of Reeds, the waters did not part immediately. Moses raised his staff, and the people waited. Then one man, Nahshon, started wading into the water. The others watched in horror as he waded in all the way up to his neck. Only then did the sea began to part, and the others rushed after him.

Perhaps this is the story Goethe was thinking of when he wrote his famous couplet:

> Whatever you can do or dream you can, begin it.
> Boldness has genius, power, and magic in it.

24

The Enemy Called Fear

AFTER ESCAPING THE EGYPTIAN PURSUIT, WITNESSING numerous miracles as they traversed the desert, receiving the Ten Commandments, and building the sanctuary, the Israelites at last find themselves at the gateway to the Promised Land. One might assume they would enter eagerly. After all, so far God has delivered on every promise He has made, and this is the climax of their journey. But no. Suspicious and fearful, they hesitate.

They are afraid—afraid of the unknown—even though God Himself has told them that the next stop is a bountiful land, flowing with milk and honey. Thus the Bible, yet again, takes up the lesson of insecurity.

We have discussed the evils that emanate from insecurity in Chapter 11, when we examined the insecurities of the pharaoh, and again in Chapters 13 and 17, when we examined the insecurities of the newly freed slaves. Remember that the Israelites even built a golden calf when, in the absence of their leader, Moses, their insecurities got the best of them.

In this story, the slave mentality surfaces once more. Not long ago, these people cowered before their masters; here again, they tremble before the unknown. Thus, rather than plunging ahead, they decide to send spies to check out what lies ahead.

Twelve men, one representative from each of the twelve tribes, are selected. We are told that these men are highly regarded people—chieftains, leaders, princes. This is the House of Representatives of the nation of Israel, if you will. The names of these duly elected men are inscribed in the Bible for eternity, because the outcome of their mission will, as we shall see, have extremely dire consequences for the entire people.

The first lesson of this story lies in the selection of the spies. These are the people upon whose reports the nation will rely for its next crucial step. These people must be extremely trustworthy; the future depends on their perceptions and advice. They must be chosen carefully.

We all have made such a choice. In our youth, each one of us has undoubtedly chosen someone to trust, someone to ask for advice on the road to adulthood. We have all asked someone, directly or indirectly, "What do I have to look forward to? What does the 'Promised Land' look like? You have been there. Tell me what to expect."

Most likely, the people to whom we have directed such questions have been our parents or grandparents, but they might also have been our teachers or other mentors.

We must be careful whom we choose to be a mentor; at least we should be aware of how we have been affected by our choice. Our advisers' perceptions, whether coming from a place of courage or fear, have influenced our decisions and still shape our futures. Pity the fellow who might have trusted Macbeth's assessment: "Life . . . is a tale told by an idiot, full of sound and fury, signifying nothing."

Pity, too, those whose advisers filled their ears with negative perceptions based on their own disappointments in life, such as "You can't trust anyone" or "Everyone will cheat you sooner or later."

Ten of the spies selected by the Israelites have presumably been raised by such mentors—people who, as Egyptian slaves, have come to view life through a filter of negativity and oppression. And these spies take this attitude with them on their journey.

Starting from a location in the Sinai known as Kadesh Barnea, the spies traverse the desert of the Negev, going up to Hebron, where Abraham is buried. During their travels they come to a vineyard and cut down a branch bearing a single cluster of grapes so large that two men have to carry the branch between them; they also collect other fruits to help them describe the abundance of the land.

After a journey of forty days, the spies return to give their report, describing a rich and fertile territory, just as God had promised. However, the tone of the report soon changes. Two of the spies, Caleb and Joshua, urge the nation to march forth and lay claim to the land, but the ten others speak from fear. *"The country that we traversed and scouted is one that devours settlers,"* they claim. *"All the people we saw are giants . . . we looked like grasshoppers in our own sight."*

It's easy to imagine a modern-day parallel. Had these spies been sent to scout New York City, they would have returned talking not of the cultural attractions but of the muggings. Had they been sent to Los Angeles, they would have returned talking of riots and earthquakes. Had they ended up anywhere on the globe, they would have brought back only bad news.

Despite claims to the contrary, people everywhere love to hear bad news. The Israelites are no exceptions, so they choose to dismiss the optimistic reports of Caleb and Joshua and focus on the pessimistic reports of the others.

The world hasn't changed much since then. We still tend to focus on the negative. It is bad news that sells newspapers. It is bad news that feeds the rumor mills. Think about it. Would you be more likely to grab the phone to tell someone that your neighbor's son earned honors in college or that he was expelled for bad behavior?

The Israelites are no different. The bad news goes around the encampment like wildfire, drowning out the good news. The Bible tells us, *"The whole community broke into loud cries, and the people wept that night. All the Israelites railed against Moses and Aaron. 'If only we had died in the land of Egypt, if only we might die in this wilderness.' . . . And they said to one another . . . 'Let us head back to Egypt.' "*

Despite the exhortations of Moses and Aaron, and in spite of the best efforts of Joshua and Caleb, the people do not quiet down. In fact, they do just the opposite: They threaten to stone those who are urging them to be calm and to trust in God.

Can the grip of fear be so strong that it causes us to abandon all faith and reason? I think the history of humanity stands as proof that this is so. Indeed, some of the best-selling New Age thinkers have posited that fear is the cause of all evil in the world. Fear leads nations to build up arsenals and go to war against other nations. Fear leads wealthy people to hoard their wealth, lest poverty strike. Fear tells us that there is never enough power or money to shield us from the unknown future.

Yet the Israelites have witnessed countless miracles; they know they have the unlimited help of God; they have made a covenant with the Creator of the world. So how can they suddenly be so utterly faithless? How can they, who have heard the very voice of God, so easily defy Him?

Herman Wouk, in his classic work *This Is My God,* explains this slave mentality:

> Economists know that, contrary to the popular impression, slaves do not work hard. . . . Take away a man's rights to him-

self, and he becomes dull and sluggish, wily and evasive, a master of the arts of avoiding responsibility and expending little energy. . . . The lash stings a slave who has halted dumbly, out of indifference and inertia, into resuming the slothful pace of his fellow slaves. It can do no more. The slave's life is a dog's life, degraded, but not wearying, and—for a broken spirit—not unpleasant. Broken by slavery, [the Israelites] could not shake free of improvidence, cowardice, and idol-worship.

This is why, Wouk suggests, they were so eager to return to Egypt every time the slightest thing went wrong. Slavery, in retrospect, did not seem all that terrible. Their spirit degraded and broken through years of slavery, the Israelites could not recover their self-esteem as free people. They totally lacked confidence that they could make a life for themselves, *even with the help of God.*

However, God clearly expects them to rise above the traumatic experiences they endured in Egypt. He has given them all the necessary help. He has met them more than halfway. With signs and miracles, He has led them to the edge of the Promised Land. All they have to do is cross over. But overcome with insecurity and fear, they cannot—or will not—take this next step.

How many of us, burdened by traumatic childhood experiences, choose to bemoan our fate, blaming our parents and God rather than taking advantage of the window of opportunity to cross over to the new approach to life offered by the Promised Land? How many people refuse to take a risk and embrace life, preferring, it seems, to lead lives of quiet desperation? In my profession, I meet such people every day. For them, it is more comfortable to be a slave than to step boldly into the unknown.

One of my clients, a young man born into wealth, had been warned by his father not to trust women. All women were "gold diggers" who would chase him for his money, claimed the father, a man who had apparently been disappointed in love. Fortunately, this man was able to overcome the fear that had kept him a slave to his father's negativity. When he dated, he took great pains to pretend that he was struggling financially, and thus he was able to make certain that his dates could not be chasing after his money. Eventually, when he did meet a woman he wanted to marry, he felt he could trust her enough to reveal and explain his deception. She forgave him readily, and the story had a fairy-tale ending.

Unfortunately, the story of another client, a woman in her forties, has no such happy outcome. This woman was also raised in an overly protective household by a very rich father. Since his death, she has continued to be protected by a vast inheritance, and as a result she has chosen to lead a life of almost total inertia. She seems paralyzed by an inability to make even the simplest decision on her own. She shops endlessly, comparing goods and prices but buying nothing. So far, her psychological insights into her situation have not led to changes in her behavior or an alteration of her life goal, which seems to be merely to exist. Most of us get many chances to free ourselves from the burdens of the past, but as we see in this Bible story, there comes a time when the chances run out.

After forgiving time and again and providing a seemingly endless supply of chances, God closes the book on the Israelites, whom He has led out of bondage.

The ten spies responsible for speaking ill of the land and spreading panic are stricken with a plague and die. And all those who elected them will have to bear their share of the responsibility for what happened, for their lack of faith.

For *each day* of the spies' journey, the Israelites are doomed to wander in the wilderness for *one year.* For forty years, then, they are banished from the Promised Land, until all those born in Egypt have died and the slave mentality has died with them.

All is not lost, though. Joshua and Caleb, the two courageous spies, are rewarded with long lives. And it is Joshua who someday will lead a new generation to the walls of Jericho. He will order the priests to blow rams' horns and the people to shout, and the walls of Jericho—along with the other walls of the past—will come tumbling down.

25

The Goal Is the Journey

As you might imagine, the pronouncement that all the Israelites who were born in slavery—which at this point means the great majority of them—are doomed to wander for forty years and die in the desert is hard for them to accept. They are intimidated by the power of God, but within a short time the now familiar grumbling begins anew: Why did we ever leave Egypt? Why should we die in the wilderness? And so on and so forth.

It is out of such discontent that revolutions are born, and sure enough, before long there arises a Lenin-to-be. His name is Korah. He is Moses's first cousin, and as such, he is a Levite, a member of the priestly class. But Korah wants to be *chief* priest.

We have already seen in Chapter 19 what happened to the sons of Aaron, who had similarly high ambitions. But Korah seems to have a short memory. So here again, the Bible takes up the perils of desire, covetousness, and envy. These unfortunate human failings are things with which we must struggle, a struggle begun back in the Garden of Eden.

You might recall that the snake seduced Eve into tasting of the tree of knowledge of good and evil by suggesting that God had forbidden it so that she and Adam would not become equal to Him: *"God knows that in the day you eat of it, your eyes will be opened and you will be like a divine being."* Coveting God-like powers, Eve bites.

As Eve's descendants, we must overcome this tendency, and that is a very tough assignment. All of us have experienced feelings of envy, and we have witnessed those whose lives have been consumed by it. We have all read of drawn-out cases in which siblings go to their graves still contesting their parents' wills, unwilling to let one have a greater share of the estate than the others. We have all read of movie stars whose marriages end up on the rocks when one spouse achieves greater fame than the other.

I am reminded of John Donne's poem in which he names a long list of things that are impossible for a human being to achieve:

> Go, and catch a falling star,
> Get with child a mandrake root,
> Tell me, where all past years are,
> Or who cleft the devil's foot,
> Teach me to hear mermaids singing,
> Or to keep off envies stinging . . .

If we buy Donne's view, we have about as much chance of overcoming envy as we do of catching a falling star or hearing mermaids sing. But the Bible holds a different view. It not only says we *can* overcome envy; it says we *must*. The story of Korah is yet another in a long list of admonitions in this regard.

Korah seizes upon the discontent of the people as a golden opportunity to challenge Moses's power. His bold move feeds into the envious feelings of some 250 chieftains, leaders, and princes, who join the revolution. But as we might recall, chieftains, leaders, and princes also misled the crowd into thinking that the Promised Land could not be entered because of the giants living there. Is the Bible telling us to be wary of leaders and politicians? Perhaps.

The basis of Korah's rebellion is very clever: He uses Moses's own words against him, twisting them around and throwing them into his face. In this regard, he is not unlike the thousands of false prophets who have arisen throughout history. These charismatic leaders typically have taken deep truths, twisted them to serve their own purposes, and managed to get a lot of unfortunate people to follow them, usually with disastrous results. Perhaps it is the similarity in the names that brings to mind the latest such example: that of David Koresh and his cult of Branch Davidians who met a fiery death in Waco, Texas.

Korah says that Moses has no right to lord over the people, since, as Moses himself has declared, God considers the Israelites *"a holy nation."* Along with the other rebels, Korah challenges Moses: *"You take too much upon you, seeing all those in the congregation are holy, every one of them."*

Moses can't believe his ears. Unlike Korah, Moses has an excellent memory. Yes, God wanted the Israelites to be His holy nation; that is why He made a covenant with them and gave them the Ten Commandments. But Moses remembers very well that since then they have not acted much like a holy nation, and thus a series of disasters has befallen them.

Moses remembers the golden calf and God's subsequent anger. He remembers the constant whining and the paralyzing lack of faith that have beset the Israelites on their journey. And what is foremost in his mind is that just a short time ago, after the Israelites' faith crumbled yet again following the report of the spies, they were condemned to wander in the desert for forty years! How can Korah call this the behavior of a holy nation? He seems to be exhibiting a colossal case of the most overused human defense mechanism: denial.

Faced with the prospect of spending the rest of his life in the wilderness, Korah, rather than repenting and making the best of the journey, says, in effect, Who needs the Promised Land anyway? We are already holy. Why bother to strive for anything better or higher?

Korah's attitude is often seen today when we confront the so-called midlife crisis. Occurring at approximately age forty, it is the time when most of us must face our mortality. We have passed the middle point of our lives, judging by current life expectancies. Often, by this time, someone near and dear to us has died. We must reevaluate who we are.

I personally faced such an earthshaking realization when a rabbinic colleague of mine was diagnosed with a terminal illness and eventually died. We had gone to school together, we had gotten married about the same time, and we had approximately the same number of children, of about the same age. I knew that "there but for the grace of God go I."

For many people, the realization that we are mortal can be very painful. We now ask ourselves how many more years we have left. We evaluate what we have accomplished in life and are forced to be realistic about what we still might hope to accomplish. We realize we will never become the president of the company; we will never win an Oscar or the Pulitzer Prize. But what counts is how we respond to this crisis, to this realization that we may never reach the Promised Land in our lifetime.

Some of us respond like Korah. We sink into denial, put blinders on, and say, "I don't need to alter my life or do anything differently. I like things just as they are, and I will rebel against anyone who tries to tell me otherwise."

Others of us learn that even if we never reach the Promised Land, *how* we travel for the rest of the journey is what counts.

One woman I know who came to this understanding told me

that she had sat down and evaluated all her friendships. She had asked herself who had helped her be a better person and who had brought out the worst in her. Her evaluation completed, she had discarded most of her friends, focusing on those people who helped her make the most of her journey.

Another wonderful example I know of comes from a book by Eric Blau entitled *Common Heroes,* a series of profiles of the terminally ill. In the book, one "hero," Linda Zarins, a woman suffering from Lou Gehrig's disease, talks about the importance of appreciating life and living it to the fullest. Her hope of dying "in the saddle," so to speak, illustrates her attitude, showing that despite the gravity of her illness, she continues to have a sense of humor: "If I'm lucky," she says, "I'll choke on a croissant. If I'm not lucky, I'll be in the hospice on a lot of Valium and just go under."

It is not surprising that the midlife crisis causes many people to take another look at the religion of their childhood, which they perhaps abandoned in young adulthood, or to search for a new religion that offers them a more personal relationship with God. But it is important to realize that the search for spirituality, for a higher state of being, is just like the journey to the Promised Land. The goal is the journey. The goal is the process.

Maimonides addressed this issue in his classic *Guide for the Perplexed,* using the analogy of inhabitants of a kingdom, some of whom are trying to reach the palace of the king and some of whom are not.

Those who travel "abroad," he explains, symbolize the people who have no interest in religion. Those who arrive with their backs to the palace are pursuing false doctrines through which they will not reach God. Those who do not know how to enter the palace are those who observe religion in a rote manner, never understanding the spirit of what they practice. In his metaphor, it is only those who search for deep, mystical truth who manage to make it past the entrance hall and reach the presence of the king.

It is an ambitious challenge, this journey toward the Promised

Land. And Korah misses the point altogether. When God called the Israelites *"a holy nation,"* He anticipated their transgressions and faithlessness. Thus He did not say, "You are a holy nation" but *"you shall be . . . a holy nation."* Specifically, right before giving the Ten Commandments, God said, *"Now then, if you will obey Me faithfully and keep My covenant, you shall be My treasured possession among all the people . . . you shall be a kingdom of priests and a holy nation."* After the sanctuary is built, the message is repeated: *"You shall be holy, for I, the Lord your God, am holy."*

What does that mean, you shall be holy? What does it say about the state of humanity?

It means we must act in a certain way, striving toward a standard of behavior that is God's ideal for us. The Bible calls this being "holy," but if the language sounds archaic to you, think of it as being in tune or in balance with God and His world. Think of becoming one with nature, with your fellow human beings, with the universe, with God. Not one of us has reached the point or we wouldn't be here on earth. We are here for this purpose. We are here to live out this struggle, this dynamic, this process. We are here to try to become holy, as God is holy.

Another tough assignment? You bet. Nearly impossible? Probably. Impossible? Not according to the Bible. This assignment might defeat us if we hadn't already learned that the journey is not a linear progression but a journey of cycles. Sometimes we are ascending, sometimes descending. But we are always moving.

Korah tried to claim the opposite. He tried to stand still. But to stand still is to die. And the Bible illustrates this in no uncertain terms.

Korah and his 250 chieftains offer a burnt sacrifice to God. When they do so, the earth swallows Korah and fire consumes his followers. The Bible makes its point dramatically: *"Scarcely had {Moses} finished speaking all these words when the ground under them burst asunder, and the earth opened its mouth and swallowed them up with their households, all Korah's people and their possessions. They went down alive into Sheol, with all that belonged to them; the earth closed up over them and they vanished from the midst of the congregation. . . . And fire went forth from the Lord and consumed the two hundred and fifty men offering the incense."*

Yet, just as after a storm a rainbow lights the sky, so God, in His limitless forgiveness, shows the Israelites another way toward atonement and self-cleansing. This next story is as fascinating as it is puzzling. Yet, like everything else in the Bible, it points to startling modern-day parallels.

26

The Wounded Healer

*T*HE LORD SPOKE TO MOSES AND AARON . . . 'INSTRUCT THE IS-
raelite people to bring you a perfect red heifer without blemish ' "
Thus begins a passage that has confounded biblical scholars: the
mystery of the red cow, a creature that is now extinct. Its ashes, it
is said, had the power to heal a person who had been contaminated
through contact with a dead body. Yet strangely enough, the *kohanim*—the priests—who performed the elaborate ritual of gathering the ashes, dissolving them in fresh water, and sprinkling
them on the contaminated person would themselves become contaminated in the process.

Rabbi J. H. Hertz, in his commentary to the Soncino Press edition of the Bible, writes:

> This ordinance is the most mysterious rite in the Scripture,
> the strange features of which are duly enumerated by the Rab-
> bis. . . . "It purifies the impure, and at the same time renders im-

pure the pure!" So inscrutable was its nature—they said—that even King Solomon in his wisdom despaired of learning the secret meaning of the Red Heifer regulations.

This is a profound paradox—the person who heals becomes wounded by the experience. What are we to make of this lesson? Let us first look at the biblical context in which this mysterious passage appears and then draw some modern parallels.

As we recall from the last two chapters, the Israelites have not had much to celebrate lately. They have been doomed to wander in the desert for forty years, watching as the slaves who left Egypt die off one by one. (Already they have witnessed the first series of tragic deaths, when the earth swallowed up the rebel Korah and his followers.) There would not be much to look forward to: the harshness of the wilderness . . . death after death . . . burial after burial . . . grief . . . despair.

We need to understand the implications of this state of mind in order to make sense of our biblical puzzle. Why is it that death causes us to despair? Obviously, we mourn the loss of someone near and dear to us. But despair has another, deeper root.

I suggest that the death of anyone close to us, and frequently even someone not so close, causes us to confront our own mortality. And that confrontation leaves us with one inescapable conclusion, consciously or unconsciously realized. Having relished our exercise of free will, we suddenly realize that in death we have no choice. In death, free will is an illusion. A power beyond us—a power we are fond of calling "fate"—grabs the controls we thought we held. We realize that we are not only mortal but powerless.

Such a feeling of powerlessness might lead one to abandon any further exercise of free will. In a nation of Israelites who were prone to moaning and groaning at the slightest difficulty, it could lead to mass hysteria. One can easily imagine a Jonestown-style self-annihilation taking place. Yet at this precise time, God offers an antidote to the contamination of death, grief, and despair. The rite involves the mixing of ashes and water, the ashes symbolizing death and the water representing life.

The priest who administers the rite must himself be a very pure, very spiritual person. He is required to spend seven days before the ceremony in private retreat, contemplating the cycles of life and death—both the wounds of life and the healing aspects of life. It is essential that he muster all his inner strength for the experience, because it will transform the person he seeks to cure, as well as himself. One will walk away cured, the other wounded.

This is the paradox that even King Solomon said could not be understood. Can we possibly find a way of understanding it when King Solomon himself could not?

I suggest that maybe we can.

Obviously, our mind cannot grasp this paradox of a defiled person becoming pure by the very act that defiles the healer. An incomprehensible transformation takes place, with purity and impurity by implication blending into one—a union of opposites. This is what King Solomon said could not be *understood;* it can only be *experienced!*

The encounter between an ailing person and a healer is a mystery. What happens beneath the surface of the bodies, down deep at the level of the souls, we can never know through logic or reason. We can access it only through experience.

Not long ago, an exceptional collection of photographs, *The Power to Heal: Ancient Arts and Modern Medicine,* depicting healers all over the world, was published. In the introduction, one of the book's editors, Phillip Moffitt, wrote of "the beautiful and mysterious power that one human being can have on another through the mere act of caring."

Most of us have had such an experience in our lives. We have encountered modern examples of *kohanim:* caring doctors, psychotherapists, social workers, health care workers, and clergy.

A student in my Bible class told me that what she most remembered from nearly three years in therapy with a very able psychologist was not so much his words of advice but the atmosphere of warmth, acceptance, and healing he created. She remembered going into his office troubled, confused, and nervous and leaving calm, peaceful, and energized to take on the challenges of the day.

She hardly gave a thought, however, to the fact that her inner turmoil had not just disappeared into thin air; it had had to be absorbed and diffused by her therapist. Would it be a wonder to learn that he, too, had been changed by the encounter? Would he not have taken some of her anxiety or anger into his own life?

It's no wonder that constant contact with human negativity in the form of disease, neurosis, social maladaptation, or other behaviors causes many of our modern-day *kohanim* to burn out. We expect our healers to be healthy at all times. To be so, they must work hard on their own psychological and spiritual well-being. Some are religious people; others make a point of taking regular retreats or vacations to reconstitute their energies. I even know of a few who maintain their connection to the life force by breeding animals. One breeds dogs; another raises exotic chickens and ducks.

But healers are only people, and they, too, are subject to human frailties. One of my friends, a physician, was recently hospitalized for routine surgery. When I visited him, he said, "By the way, when you see me back next week doing rounds, please don't ask how I'm doing."

Puzzled by the request, I asked why.

"It's bad for business," he joked. Then he added, "My patients expect me to be healthy all the time."

I thought about what he had said, and I realized how true it was. Surely, none of us would want to consult a physician we knew was battling a terminal illness, such as cancer. We would be afraid that he or she would not have enough of what it takes to cure us. After all, to cure us, the doctor must give us some of his or her own life force—that is the Biblical lesson.

The famed psychotherapist C. G. Jung experienced a dramatic personal example of this process following a heart attack. He almost died, but he was brought back to life by the efforts of his physician, identified by his biographer only as "Dr. H." Later, Jung had a dream that confirmed that he had survived solely because of Dr. H. Then, on the day Jung got out of bed, Dr. H took ill. Shortly thereafter, Dr. H. died.

It should come as no surprise that immediately following the instructions concerning the red heifer, Aaron, the high priest, also dies.

It takes a special person to be a healer. One should not aspire to this profession lightly. Indeed, if we draw a parallel between modern-day healers and the biblical *kohanim*, we gain some interesting insights. God's reaction to those who would usurp the position (Korah and the sons of Aaron) clearly illustrates that those who are not called by God to this duty, but who come to it with selfish motives, are likely to suffer dire consequences. Being a healer is a special privilege that involves tremendous risk and responsibility, since the healer, as we have seen, takes on the suffering of other people. This paradox is at the core of the healing process.

ANOTHER ASPECT OF THIS PARADOX IS ILLUSTRATED BY THE BIBLICAL tale that follows the story of the red heifer.

Again, some of the Israelites are complaining. This time, they are impatient because they must travel out of their way to go around the land of Edom, which won't grant them passage. They are punished for their complaints: Poisonous snakes attack them, and many people die.

When Moses prays to God for forgiveness, he is instructed to fashion a snake out of brass, so that people can look at it and be healed. *"And Moses made a serpent of brass, and set it upon the pole; and it came to pass, that if a serpent had bitten any man, when he looked upon the serpent of brass, he lived."*

This is, of course, the archetypal symbol of healing, the caduceus, that we see on medical signs and shields. But why a snake?

First, a snake is a creature that symbolizes the transformative aspects of healing. It is a creature that hibernates, approaching a near-death state. Then, when it returns to life, it sheds its skin, physically demonstrating its inner transformation.

Second, the poison of the snake symbolizes the power of many of the medications we take, which are themselves poisonous. In large quantities, many drugs would kill us; in small quantities, they heal. This is particularly true of chemotherapy, used in treating cancer. A patient is given large quantities of highly poisonous substances, drugs that will make him or her very ill, causing vomiting, hair loss, and other side effects. But if the chemotherapy works, it poisons the cancer also and thus allows the patient to live.

Third, we have to acknowledge the snake—the dark side within each of us—before we can be cured. In order to eliminate toxicity from our lives, we must first recognize and confront it.

Fourth, we must remember that all the stories in the Bible are related to one another. It was the serpent who played a major role in seducing Adam and Eve into choosing the tree of death over the tree of life. But here we are told that the serpent can also be an agent of healing. That which hurts also has the power to heal. This is the core of the lesson: that everything on this earth has a purpose; everything can be used for good.

Even in the worst of circumstances, God does not abandon His creations. Even in the worst of circumstances, when we are drowning as a result of a choice we have made, God throws out a lifeline. But it is up to us to reach for it.

There is a joke about a man who is praying fervently, asking God to help him win the lottery. After he has been praying for a long time, God speaks to him and says, "Listen, I'll help you. But meet me halfway. Buy a ticket!"

So buy a ticket to a better life. Give God a chance. If you are ill, this is the one sure way to move toward healing. Not everyone can be cured, but one thing is guaranteed: Everyone can make the journey toward healing.

27

Home Is Where the Heart Is

THE ISRAELITES ARE NOW IN THE FINAL YEARS OF THEIR journey. They have made their way north, following the eastern shore of the Dead Sea, and are encamped in the land of Moab. From here they will eventually cross the river Jordan to enter the Promised Land.

During their wanderings, they have had numerous encounters with enemy peoples, but by and large they have prevailed. With the slave generation dying out, they are now a young, strong people.

Balak, the king of Moab, is no fool. He does not want to wage war against a force such as the Israelites. He decides not to send his soldiers against them; instead, he sends a powerful sorcerer named Balaam. Balak reasons that the right kind of spell laid on by Balaam will render the Israelites defenseless.

But Balaam is not just any sorcerer. He is a prophet who talks with God. And when it comes time to pronounce the curse, Balaam instead pronounces a blessing. It is a long blessing, and it contains these famous words: *"How goodly are your tents, O Jacob, your dwelling places, O Israel!"* This blessing has become a permanent part of Jewish prayer books; it is with these words that the daily prayer service in a synagogue begins.

I vividly recall, as a child, attending Yeshiva Rabbi Samson Raphael Hirsch in Washington Heights, New York. At the beginning of the religious services, Rabbis Joseph Breuer and Simon Schwab would enter the synagogue. As the congregation would rise to honor them, the rabbis would be reciting these beautiful words of Balaam. As I witnessed this scene over and over, it gradually became clear to me that these words of a non-Jewish prophet, recited daily in the synagogue, are there to remind everyone that there is only one God for all the people in the world.

But what does Balaam's blessing really mean? Why was Balaam so taken with the Israelites' homes? And why should it matter to us today?

In the desert, the people lived in tents. Yet the doors of the tents were positioned so that they did not face one another. This was because the Israelites respected one another. They recognized that when dwelling in close proximity to one's neighbor, it is essential to ensure privacy. Without privacy, true intimacy between husband and wife, both emotional and sexual, cannot flourish.

Privacy allows a person who returns home after a long day at work to shed his or her public persona at the door, to be free to show frailties and vulnerabilities, because only the loved one, the trusted one, will see them. The wounded healer can come home and reconstitute himself or herself in a peaceful environment, with no fear of being seen by neighbors without the "priestly robes," the work uniform.

Would that we could adapt the desert lifestyle to our times. Would that a doctor or a lawyer or a CEO could truly leave his or her work, along with the work persona, *at work,* and come home to face his or her spouse as just another frail, vulnerable human being.

Would that the home could be a place for strengthening one's inner self, rather than just another game board on which to make power plays.

One brilliant surgeon I know had grown accustomed to wielding authority and always having his way. His work had put a great deal of responsibility onto his shoulders and, unfortunately, the stress had translated into an intimidating personality. All the nurses, technicians, and medical assistants constantly deferred to him. Once, after a tough day at the hospital, he returned home still wearing his white coat, and with it his work persona, which he usually managed to stow in his locker at the hospital. This is what happened, and this is the lesson he learned.

He asked his wife to tell him the whereabouts of one of their children. When she didn't respond as quickly or exactly as he would have liked, he snapped at her just as he did at the operating room staff.

"Listen," she shot back, "maybe you can get away with talking like that to people at the hospital. But you can just leave that attitude right there at the front door!"

Through the argument that followed, the doctor learned a great deal. He also came to question his attitude at the hospital. While changes were not immediately evident, he gradually came to treat both his fellow workers and his family with more respect.

A home where you can be yourself serves as a marvelous attitude adjuster. On the other hand, a home that adds to your stresses only serves to worsen your public persona, thus negatively affecting your role in the community. It is sad but true that when something is amiss in your "tent," that negativity is often projected into your public life as well.

Balaam saw the Israelite community at its best. There was respect for neighbors' privacy. There were intimacy and love in the home life. And those virtues were brought forward into the life of the community, which radiated unity and cohesion.

It is interesting that the Hebrew word for "your dwellings," *mishkenotecha,* has the same root as the word for the Divine Presence, *Shekhinah.* Balaam saw the presence of God among these people.

Happiness at home enables you to open your heart to God much more easily. But if you are unhappy at home, the struggle with God becomes more difficult. I have noticed such a pattern among my clients and patients.

The relationship one has with his or her parents often serves as a model for one's relationship with God. If a father was highly demanding and authoritative, the child, even as an adult, tends to see God as a demanding, authoritative figure. If the childhood experience was nurturing and warm, the adult sees God as a loving being.

"Home is where the heart is," goes the saying, and it couldn't be more true. The heart dwells in the home, is loved in the home, and is broken in the home. Home is where the life experience and the God experience begin.

So the Israelites, after their many failings and transgressions, finally show that they can do something right! But the Bible wouldn't be the Bible if this happy story ended here. We know that the Bible is a story of people's struggles with God and with themselves, so all is never blissful for long.

After Balaam's blessing, the king of Moab is furious, but he goes his way. War is averted. In fact, relations between the Israelites and the Moabites become close. Too close. Soon the Israelite men are sleeping with the Moabite women, who are undoubtedly very attractive and, we are told, sexually promiscuous.

The Moabite attitude toward sex was dictated by their religion, which called for worshiping the "natural" drives of man. To pay homage to their god, Baal Peor, one simply did what came naturally, be it kill, steal, or commit adultery. The height of worship was performing the most natural act of all, defecation, before the altar. Obviously, this religion's teachings were antithetical to the teachings the Israelites had received at Mount Sinai. Yet some of the Israelites were seduced. How could that be? Because sex is a powerful human drive. But having sex with wanton abandon and lust, indulging one's base drive, eventually brings one closer to idolatry. It is no accident that the Hebrew word for "sanctity of marriage," *kidushin,* and the Hebrew word for "harlot," *kedeshah,* have the same root. Sex can take one in the direction of either sanctity or sin. There are two key differences: your mind-set and your partner.

Looking for true intimacy with the right partner will lead, it is hoped, to *kidushin* and the experience of moving onward and upward in your journey. But looking for a wild night with a *kedeshah* can earn you only a fleeting pleasure, followed by a grim morning after.

So it should not be surprising that after some wild nights with the Moabite women, the Israelite men are enticed into participating in the repulsive idolatrous practices of Baal Peor. Of course, disaster is sure to follow. As a consequence of the idol worship, a plague enters the beautiful tents of the House of Jacob, killing 24,000 people. In no uncertain terms, God is saying that curses and plagues come not from outside but from inside. An outsider, such as Balak or Balaam, can try to curse you, but he will not succeed. The only kind of curse that succeeds is the kind you bring on yourself.

Then one of the idol worshipers commits a sin so public that the priest Pinhas cannot remain still any longer. The man brings one of the loose women over to his companions *"in the sight of Moses and in the sight of the whole Israelite community, who were weeping at the entrance of the Tent of Meeting,"* the Bible relates. Pinhas kills them both, and the plague ends.

The plague had created yet another reason to grieve and despair. I would imagine that it must have become hard for many a woman to light candles on Friday night.

A woman client recently told me that she has stopped lighting candles to welcome the Sabbath, a ritual she had followed all her married life. When I asked why, I learned of the great darkness in her home resulting from her rapidly failing marriage. Yet the Bible tells us that, even after so many struggles and disasters, it is possible to bring light, to have hope. There were many more good Israelites than there were those who sank to the moral level of the gutter. And the good people kept alive the vision of the Promised Land.

This is the last lesson of the beautiful tents of Jacob: Have hope. Hope means overcoming the darkness of current reality long enough to gain a vision of a better world. Light a candle, look up at the moon, and realize that this, too, will pass and that, with the help of God, we can all journey onward and upward.

28

Cities of Refuge

We HAVE NOW COME TO THE END OF THE BOOK OF Numbers, the fourth of the Five Books of Moses. What follows in the fifth book, the Book of Deuteronomy, is Moses's farewell to his people, which essentially recaps the major lessons of their forty years in the wilderness. In the remaining chapters, we will take a careful look at the unusual choices Moses makes.

But at this juncture we must recognize that the key teachings of how to live an ethical life end here. Therefore, we must pay extra attention to the last message God gives us.

The final passages of the Book of Numbers deal, innocuously enough, with apportionment of land. We learn that ten of the tribes—the descendants of ten of Jacob's sons—will be receiving parcels of land, as will the two tribes descended from the sons of Joseph. The tribe of Levi, which is restricted to serving as priests in the Temple, receives no land but instead is instructed to live in forty-eight different cities. Six of these receive a special and highly unusual designation: "Cities of Refuge."

These cities prove to be a unique biblical provision that is especially significant—and I cannot stress this strongly enough—because this message comes at the very end of the essential teachings.

What are these Cities of Refuge? *"These six cities,"* the Bible explains, *"shall serve for refuge, so that anyone who kills a person unintentionally may flee there."*

The Cities of Refuge were thus designated as sanctuaries for those who might accidentally take another life. The Bible is clear that an unmistakable case of murder warrants the death penalty, although even then the testimony of more than one eyewitness is required and malice must be established. But the Bible also takes great pains to ensure that places of protection exist for those who may have acted foolishly or carelessly but unintentionally.

Why would such offenders need to flee to a special place for protection? Wouldn't it have been simpler just to declare that unintentional or accidental killing is not to be punished in the same manner as intentional killing?

It might seem that such a prescription would be simpler, but the Bible is a great deal wiser than that. The Bible is concerned with many more things than the balanced administration of justice. For example, the Bible is concerned with the feelings of the relatives of the deceased. Their anger and grief at the waste of a loved one's life might cause them to seek revenge and commit a senseless act of violence. So the family members need to be protected from the excesses of their own emotions, and, of course, the offender needs to be protected as well.

Even if the family does not act in revenge, the presence of the guilty party would serve as a constant reminder of their loss. This would likely fuel their feelings of bitterness and hatred, causing all manner of psychological damage to those burdened with such feelings and to those with whom they interact.

The Bible also recognizes that an act of carelessness, such as one leading to a loss of life, does not happen in a vacuum. Something inside a community and/or an individual has created a climate that has led to this occurrence, or at least made it possible. The presence of such an atmosphere requires healing, which can best take place outside the community that engendered the tragic event.

A recent article in the *Los Angeles Times* brought to mind a modern-day parallel to this biblical concern. A female pedestrian was killed in a hit-and-run accident. The police tracked down the man responsible, but before they could question him, he committed suicide. He left a suicide note indicating his guilt and remorse. What I found particularly interesting was that the man responsible was a Cuban refugee who for many years had tried, without success, to bring his family and children to the United States. It was not clear which society, Cuban or American, had stymied his efforts. But his failure had apparently caused him to despair; he had lived a lonely, depressed life.

Depression is often at the root of the distraction that leads to an accidental killing. So is anxiety. Both lead to a self-preoccupation that causes a person not to pay attention to the outside world. Both are also related to the use of alcohol and drugs, which are often involved when accidents occur.

Another significant factor in accidents is fatigue. Statistics reveal that industrial accidents are frequently caused by workers who are overworked or exhausted. Truck drivers, for example, may get into accidents after they have been driving for too long without adequate sleep.

What is happening here? Why are people working so hard, pushing themselves past their limits, so that they end up taking the lives of others? There are two possible explanations, each of which puts the blame on both the individual and the community. Say, for example, some family members have been irresponsible and accumulated high credit card bills, which the breadwinner is now pushing hard to pay off. Yes, it's the fault of the big spenders, but some blame also belongs to their community, which places such a high value on material acquisitions and tempts people, through promotions and advertising, to spend beyond their means.

Another scenario is that a family has been very responsible and thrifty, but its resources have been eaten up by a major illness. If one member of the family pushes beyond his or her limits in an effort to make ends meet under such circumstances, we have to ask: What is wrong with the immediate community that it does not help out? What is wrong with the larger society that there is no medical insurance structure for people caught in such dire straits?

Thus, the Bible sees clearly that blame cannot easily be assigned in cases of accidental death, and it makes provisions for healing.

Another factor the Bible takes into account is the burden of guilt felt by the unfortunate offender and how this guilt is likely to affect his or her life. In the newspaper story I cited above, the man responsible simply could not live with his guilt and committed suicide. In other instances, guilt can be so great that it can lead to a nervous breakdown or other tragedies.

One of my clients, an excellent physician, accidentally caused the death of a patient through poor judgment. Although medical authorities absolved him of malpractice, he knew in his heart that he had been responsible. The guilt ate away at him constantly, rendering him incapable of practicing medicine.

Another case with which I am familiar involved a mother whose child drowned while she was sitting by the pool, engrossed in a conversation with friends. The fact that she had been so close yet had not been paying attention, the fact that she could so easily have prevented the death of her child, plunged her into such a deep depression that she has been totally ineffectual in caring for her surviving children.

Both these people needed a City of Refuge, where they could have dealt with their guilt and found healing.

SO WHAT WAS SUPPOSED TO HAPPEN INSIDE THE CITIES OF REFUGE? Remember that each City of Refuge belonged to the tribe of Levi—the tribe of priests, of teachers, of a very spiritual people who had been appointed the moral leaders of the Israelites.

Thus, the offender was not sent to a prison as we know it; rather, he was sent to a "holy" city of priestly people who would not condemn him but would protect him and help him find his way back.

The most significant aspect of a City of Refuge was that it was, in every meaning of the word, a sanctuary. A sanctuary is, of course, a place of protection. But a sanctuary is also a temple to God—designed and built according to God's instructions and cared for by priests.

In Chapter 17, we discussed God's instruction to Moses to build a symbol of His presence among the Israelites: *"And build for Me a sanctuary so that I may dwell among them."* We learned that the sanctuary was not meant as a house for God. God had *not* said "And build for Me a sanctuary so that I may dwell *in it"* but *"And build for Me a sanctuary so that I may dwell among them."* Here, at the very end of the Book of Numbers, we are again reminded what a sanctuary is.

A sanctuary—be it a temple of marble and gold or a City of Refuge to which criminals flee—is a powerful, concrete symbol of God's constant presence among people. God dwells with people, whoever they are, whatever they have done. His covenant with them is unshakable: His love is unconditional. No matter who you are and what you have done, God does not abandon you. God recognizes that people make mistakes. He always gives us another chance. And this is what the hapless offender—ridden with guilt and remorse—was to learn in the City of Refuge.

Surrounded by priestly people who were compassionate, who set the best possible example, and who could guide him along a path toward rehabilitation, the offender could gain insight into his behavior, atone for his sin, and learn to raise his head again.

Yet he could not return from the City of Refuge until the high priest died. This is another interesting biblical instruction that may seem puzzling. But remember that the nation of Israelites had no king or monarch. The high priest was the highest, most visible leader, comparable to the president of the United States.

As leader, he was responsible for all that went right and wrong with his people. He represented the collective interest, and the senseless waste of life through an accidental killing should have served as a warning to him. Perhaps he was not leading his people in the best way. Perhaps he should have instituted necessary programs or prayed in a different way. On some level the high priest had failed, and the person who personified his failure was sent away while the high priest mended the fabric of the society. The high priest's death signified that his task was finished.

When the high priest died, the nation mourned. Then, following a period of mourning, a new cycle of life could begin. And the offender, who had been secluded in introspective study, could return to the public realm. So again the Bible tells us, as it has so many times, that life is made up of cycles—of birth and death, of good and bad, of private intimacy and public celebration.

King Solomon summed up this lesson most beautifully in his writings:

> *A season is set for everything,*
> *A time for every experience under heaven:*
> *A time for being born and a time for dying,*
> *A time for planting and a time for uprooting the planted;*
> *A time for slaying and a time for healing . . .*

Each time has its purpose, but there are constants that are timeless: God's presence, His compassion, His kindness. These endure forever. And that is the last lesson of the Book of Numbers.

PART V

29

Listening and Hearing

OSES KNOWS HE IS GOING TO DIE. HE KNOWS that he, like the generation of slaves he has led out of Egypt, will not be crossing the river Jordan into the Promised Land. And he wants to make certain that all the young people who were born after the momentous events on Mount Sinai understand what happened there.

So he sits down and writes his farewell address, which he will deliver to this new generation. This is the fifth book of Moses, the Book of Deuteronomy, so named by English translators after the Greek word for "repetition." Moses endeavors to ensure that these words will have a lasting impact, knowing that words of parting are perhaps remembered best.

Indeed, Moses is right. Some of the best-remembered and most enduring works of literature are speeches of farewell. Who has not been struck by the parting speech that Polonius makes to his son in *Hamlet*: "Give each man thy ear but few thy voice . . . Neither a borrower nor a lender be . . . This above all—to thine own self be true." Many people have told me that the words of farewell spoken on a deathbed by a parent or a loved one have stayed with them forever.

So this is Moses's last will and testament, but it is much more than what we think of as a last will and testament today. And it is far more eloquent than Shakespeare. He calls the young Israelites together and asks them to listen and to hear. He could not be more adamant about this. In the Book of Deuteronomy, the words "hear" and "listen" appear more than seventy times.

To listen is to become open and attentive to the words that reach our ears. To hear is to allow them to penetrate into our minds and hearts. And this is what Moses is calling upon his people to do when he begins, *"Hear, O Israel, the laws and rules that I proclaim to you this day! Study them and observe them faithfully!"*

He continues, *"The Lord our God made a covenant with us at Horeb {Mount Sinai}. It was not with our fathers that the Lord made this covenant, but with us, the living, every one of us who is here today."*

How could that be? After all, most of those to whom Moses is speaking weren't even born at the time of the revelation at Mount Sinai. That is precisely his point. God's covenant was made with those present in body, as well as with those present in soul. God spoke to the slaves who had already died, as well as to the young Israelites who followed them. So, too, He speaks to all of us today. Perhaps we have stopped listening, but the voice of God has continued to travel through time and space, striving to reach every human being ever created.

Moses knew very well that his words of farewell would be read by people born thousands of years after him. He was speaking to all of us when he said, *"The Lord our God made a covenant with us . . . every one of us who is here today."* You and me.

If you think you have never heard the voice of God, it simply means that you have never tuned in to the right frequency. Many of us cannot hear God because our heads are so busy listening to so many other voices. We hear voices of teachers who told us we would never amount to anything. We hear voices of fathers who told us we didn't matter as much as their golf games. We hear voices of mothers who told us we weren't attractive enough. We hear such voices, and we react with anger, depression, or apathy. We are so busy arguing with them that we hardly notice that we are actually arguing with our spouses, our children, or our coworkers.

We all think that people who hear voices must be psychotic. Indeed, when voices from the past take over, madness sets in. But many of us, far from being psychotic, are operating in a neurotic state, ruled by the voices of our parents or teachers.

To hear the voice of God, you must clear the airwaves. The voices of negativity that you let in cause too much static, too much interference. It takes hard work—and often some time in therapy—to focus your attention to listen. But if you are willing to do this work, the reward is great: You will hear the voice of God.

Clients and patients constantly ask me, "What does the voice of God sound like? What is it I should be listening for?" I have no answer to this question. For each individual, the experience is unique. But I can say, with a fair degree of certainty, what it does *not* sound like.

As we discussed in Chapter 3, the voice of God—with the possible exception of the event at Mount Sinai—does not boom out of the heavens, accompanied by thunder and lightning. It is a voice that comes not from the outside but from within. The prophet Elijah had an experience that taught him how God speaks to man: *"There was a great and mighty wind, splitting mountains and shattering rocks . . . but the Lord was not in the wind. After the wind was an earthquake, but the Lord was not in the earthquake. After the earthquake was fire, but the Lord was not in the fire. And after the fire was the still small voice."*

The still small voice, the voice from within, that spoke to the prophet Elijah was the voice of God.

God also speaks to us through his messengers. These messengers might be angels, as we discussed in Chapter 9, or they might be ordinary people who are totally unaware that they are conveying God's message to us.

Be alert to each person you meet and think about what message he or she may be bringing to you. Even people who cause you discomfort may be conveying an important message through their behavior.

A dramatic illustration of this process was related to me by a student of mine who took a hiking trip in the Sinai desert. Although she did not say so, she had been looking for some kind of encounter with God that would bring into focus a deeply personal aspect of her spiritual journey.

While she and a friend were camped in the wilderness, awed by the majesty of this forbidding, magical place, their peace and contemplation were disturbed by three hikers. The hikers chose that precise moment to take a rest, and even though they could have picked any place within miles, they parked themselves within ten feet of my student. She was incensed. "How could these people be so thoughtless, so insensitive to the privacy of others?" she grumbled to her friend. Then it hit her.

She remembered the biblical story of Abraham and how he interrupts his conversation with God to welcome three strangers, who turn out to be angels. She realized that, although she considered Abraham her role model, she was not behaving the least bit like him. Dramatically, she came face to face with her shadow side. She realized that both here in the Sinai and at home, she resented people who disturbed her solitude. She resented people coming to her door without calling. She resented being interrupted. She relished her privacy and lacked spontaneity.

She felt as if someone had seized her head and turned it 180 degrees. She immediately changed her attitude and was pleasant to the hikers, who moved on shortly thereafter. The experience was such a powerful lesson that she still speaks fondly of it, relating it to anyone who will listen. She went to the Sinai to meet God, and indeed she met Him, in the guise of three examples of His creation.

Another way we meet God, hear God, is through synchronicity—events that are seemingly unrelated but that coincide by more than chance. As a therapist, I have frequently witnessed this phenomenon, in which an experience with one client has a powerful impact on my work with another.

I will never forget one such instance. It involved a female client who walked into my office for the first time and immediately focused on a small hand-painted tile that had been given to me by a former client. It was a small piece of simple folk art, and I couldn't help but wonder why my new client was attracted to it. The artist had come for counseling some years earlier, during a particularly difficult time in her life, when she had been undergoing artificial insemination.

I must say that I was astonished when my new client confided that she, too, was contemplating this procedure. These were the only two women who had come to me concerning this particular issue.

I felt that God was with me. Nothing is arbitrary, and nothing happens without the guiding force of the Divine Presence. As it turned out, what I had learned through my experience with the first client proved most helpful with the second.

As a psychologist, I am also particularly interested in yet another way in which God speaks to us: through dreams. If we learn how to interpret them, the voices we hear in dreams can help to guide us and bring us insight and understanding.

Voices can emanate from many sources. Some interesting examples are cited by Dr. Brian Weiss in his book *Many Lives, Many Masters,* in which he relates the story of a client's regression to past lives. While under hypnosis, this woman heard a voice telling her to "polish her diamond." She later understood that this message referred to enhancing and protecting what she had. Perhaps this woman was too concerned with her past lives and was not taking good enough care of the life she already had. And it took a voice from the past—perhaps the voice of God—to tell her so.

The lesson I am trying to convey is that God's voice did not cease at Mount Sinai. That is what Moses is telling us. All we have to do, Moses says, is listen and hear.

Having made his point so dramatically, Moses speaks the words that have been committed to memory by all the descendants of those who heard it from his lips. It is the statement that children are meant to learn first, and it is the last statement that the dying are meant to recite before they leave this world. Moses couldn't be more ardent about it: *"You shall take to heart the words with which I charge you this day. You shall teach them diligently to your children. You shall recite them when you are at home and when you are away, when you lie down and when you rise up."*

And what are these words that Moses is urging the people to learn, to keep, to repeat?

They are the essential statement of monotheism, which Moses expresses in six Hebrew words. In English, it may sound cryptic: *"Hear, O Israel, the Eternal, our God, the Eternal is one."* But it is meant to be as simple as it sounds. It is a statement of faith, of love, and of commitment to act in accordance with God's ways. God is one. God is whole. And to live that belief means bringing oneness and wholeness into the world. It means bringing people together, bringing unity and peace into the lives we touch.

If that task seems too great for ordinary mortals—if you are asking: How am I to bring peace to a world that seems constantly at war?—look at your own life. Peace, love, wholeness, and oneness enter the world in tiny increments.

Will what you say to a friend about a mutual acquaintance foster a better friendship among all involved or serve to create suspicion and distance? Will your angry response to someone who has hurt your feelings fix the problem or make it worse?

How you relate to the microworld of your friends and family is likely to set the pattern of how you relate to the macroworld outside your immediate sphere of influence. But both must be your concern. If you care only for yourself, you have not heard the voice of God.

Rabbi Dr. Adolf (Avraham) Altmann, former chief rabbi of Trier, Germany, in his study of this biblical passage (the full text of which I have included in my book *Jewish Values in Jungian Psychology*) suggests that the ability to hear God's voice is directly related to one's actions and ethics. If one hears the call from Sinai and its quiet, daily echoes, one is obliged to act upon that divine message in a godly, ethical fashion. Rabbi Altmann writes most poignantly:

> There are voices and calls which sound out loud, yet one fails to hear them, and there are others that make no sound at all, yet they are heard. The human without ethics passes by what cries out most in life without hearing, whereas one of high moral character hears even the most subdued call and traces its source. . . . If no one else hears the silent cry of the humiliated, the powerless, hidden victims, the Jew must hear it; that is the noblest ethical significance of "Hear, O Israel."

It is clear that this message is addressed to all spiritual people who wish to hear the voice of God.

First, open your channels. Make yourself receptive to God's message. Listen. Then it will come. You will hear it. And if you have truly heard it, the voice of God will enter your mind and your heart, and your actions will testify to the fact that God dwells here, now, among us all.

30

Choices

MOSES CONTINUES, *"AND YOU SHALL LOVE THE LORD your God with all your hearts, and with all your soul, and with all you have."*

Wait a second. Did Moses say "hearts"—plural? His words in Hebrew are next to impossible to translate accurately into English. But to anyone who knows Hebrew, the Bible's unusual spelling of this word is arresting and puzzling.

The Hebrew word for "heart" consists of two letters—*l'v*—not coincidentally, I think, related in sound to the word "love." But in this passage the word is written *l'vv*.

What could that possibly mean? A human being has only one heart. What is Moses really trying to say with "all your hearts"?

Yes. In truth, he means something even deeper than that. Moses is talking about a single heart that has two sides: one in the light and one in the shadow, one inclined to good, one to evil. These two sides constantly remind human beings of their gift of free will and the inevitable struggles that accompany it. So it has been since the dawn of human history.

Even as he is speaking to the people in what is to be the final year of his life, Moses thinks back to the beginning of all that has been written in the five books. He thinks back to the story of creation.

Everything on this earth was created with a dual aspect. Ever since human beings experienced that split, they have struggled to understand both it and its reason for being. The famed philosopher Georg W. F. Hegel expressed it in terms of "thesis" and "antithesis." Hermann Hesse wrote about it beautifully in his *Narcissus and Goldmund:*

> All existence seemed to be based on duality, on contrast. Either one was a man or one was a woman, either a wanderer or a sedentary burgher, either a thinking person or a feeling person—no one could breathe in at the same time as he breathed out, be a man as well as a woman, experience freedom as well as order, combine instinct and mind. One always had to pay for the one with the loss of the other, and one thing was always just as important and desirable as the other.

This is what Moses is reminding us. At the first moment of human history, when man and woman were placed in the Garden of Eden, they were confronted with two trees—and a choice. Ever since then, such has been the human condition. Temptation—the serpent—always plays a role. And we live and die by our choices. Spiritually speaking, we choose life or death at every juncture.

We might ask, then, Why is it so hard to make the right choice, since the Bible instructs us to choose life every time? If it were that simple, it would not be a real choice. The choice the serpent presents is, on its face, always very appealing, very attractive. Only when we think about the *consequences* of following the evil inclination do we pause, and it is that pause that initiates the struggle.

No one is immune to this struggle, and no one succeeds in making the right choice each and every time. Indeed, it has been said that there is no great person who hasn't made a mistake. I would add that there is no great person who hasn't made a great mistake. This is simply because great people choose to take great risks, and implied in each great risk are choices, one or more of which are sure to lead in the wrong direction.

OFTEN THE CHOICES WE ARE CALLED ON TO MAKE ARE SUBTLE. THE evil inclination doesn't always masquerade as a seductive sex partner. Sometimes the evil inclination even masquerades as a good deed.

When a husband invites company to dinner without first checking with his wife, is he responding to the good inclination to love his neighbor or to the evil inclination to disregard his wife's feelings? Scratch the surface of a dilemma like that, and you are bound to find that the people invited to dinner were likely to advance the husband's business or perhaps that he needed to make himself feel good by his spontaneous invitation—at the expense of his wife's feelings.

In some hospitals, medical systems have recently been instituted that operate according to the concept of "managed care." In an effort to keep health care costs down, doctors are instructed to see as many patients as possible within a limited period of time, spending extra time only with those whose medical condition truly demands it. I am told that this ideal is hard to put into practice. Some doctors prefer to spend more time with patients they enjoy being with, not necessarily the sickest ones. Often the sickest ones are the most unappealing—they smell bad, they complain endlessly, they question the doctor's instructions. Often these patients are people who have neglected their health due to poverty or ignorance, and they now face many complications. The doctor ought to spend extra time with such a patient, but that is exactly the kind of patient he'd rather rush out the door. So what choice will he make?

As a psychologist, I am not immune to this dilemma. There is a joke in my profession that we would all rather work with a "YAVIS," an acronym that describes a patient who is young, attractive, verbal, intelligent, and successful. No one wants to struggle with an "OUNDUF," a patient who is old, ugly, nonverbal, dumb, and a failure. Yet quite possibly, the latter is the one who needs a psychologist more.

How do you see the good in what appears unattractive and the evil in what is sexy and seems good?

We answered that question in Chapter 21, when we discussed the concept of "love your neighbor." When you recognize and embrace that which is not so good and not so appealing within yourself, when you learn to love yourself, you will see those around you through different eyes. This is because recognizing the good and the evil inclinations has a great deal to do with how you perceive things.

Moses is well aware of this reality. Some in his audience, who have seen only the worst in everything, will never reach the Promised Land as a consequence of their complaints and lack of faith. He is well aware that many of those who will be reading his words in the generations to come will be like these people. For reasons of their own making, or perhaps due to circumstances beyond their control, they will also be far from the Promised Land. So he is trying to teach that how you see things is everything. Again, there is a choice. And the choice of what you perceive and how you perceive is yours. It is an important choice, because your perception of the reality around you determines how you will act.

I try to teach patients that the duality that defines all creation extends to reality as well. We all operate in two realities. There is the physical reality based on our five senses: touch, sight, hearing, taste, and smell. And there is the psychic reality based on our inner selves: imagination, intuition, and soul. When the physical reality is unbearable, it is possible for us to call on the psychic reality to get us through.

One of my clients, who as a child had been physically abused by her mother, told me she had understood the concept of psychic reality very early in life; she had learned it through reading fairy tales. Her physical reality might have crushed her were it not for the fact that, in her imagination, she created for herself another world, another home, with a loving, caring mother. That is how she coped.

One of the most beloved works of children's literature, *A Little Princess* by Frances Hodgson Burnett, tells the story of a young girl, Sarah, who at a time of great deprivation and poverty tells herself that she is a princess, surrounded by beauty and luxury. Because she is a princess, she must carry herself with the high self-esteem that befits her station, and she must behave with dignity in situations that are degrading to her. Sarah uses her imagination to create a psychic reality that saves her soul from despair.

To me it is interesting that Sarah possesses an object that helps her gain access to her imaginary world—her doll. Often adults have such an object: a piece of art or jewelry, a gift from someone near and dear that brings to mind a feeling or a memory that, like a key, unlocks the door to one's psychic reality.

For me, one such object is a *kiddush* cup, a silver wine cup given to me by a very special patient, the late Dr. Erwin Altman. Whenever I drink from this precious gift, I am reminded of the spiritual legacy and friendship of his entire family, as well as the inspiring words of his father, Rabbi Altmann, whose beautiful words I quoted in the last chapter.

For my mother, an immigrant from Germany, the Statue of Liberty is such an object. On her journey to the United States before World War II, the image of the Statue of Liberty reminded her of a promising future in her new homeland. Even now, that statue continues to inspire her.

For some cancer patients at the hospital where I work, such an inspirational object is a beautiful photograph that hangs outside the Oncology Department. It depicts the western wall of the Temple in Jerusalem, known also as the Wailing Wall. I have seen many a patient stand before that photograph, studying it carefully.

I know that each patient chooses what to see in it. Some see a symbol of destruction: The Temple is no more. Their body, too, is being destroyed by cancer. It is time to weep and wail, mourning what might have been. Some see a symbol of redemption. The wall represents the only remaining piece of the Temple, a place that has not been destroyed in two thousand years. By looking at this picture, a patient who chooses to enter a private psychic reality can be transported to the Promised Land.

The wonderful thing about the psychic reality is that it travels with us wherever we go. It is just as real as our physical reality. A Promised Land of the imagination has no geographic boundaries. It is not like a house, filled with many possessions, that cannot be picked up and transported along with us. Possessions can be stolen or destroyed, but the psychic reality can never be taken from us.

One of the great lessons that Moses is teaching us is that, like the psychic reality, religion is portable. The Ark of the Covenant, which held the tablets on which were written the Ten Commandments, was designed and built with handles so that it could be carried along as the people traveled through the wilderness. Even after the destruction of the Temple, when the Ark disappeared, the loss was not insurmountable. By then, everyone had committed the Ten Commandments and their meaning to memory. The words of God, as spoken to Moses, were indelibly engraved in the psychic reality of his descendants. All that remains is making the choice to access the inner sanctuary, where the Ark is stored.

SO THE POINT IS MADE: LIFE IS ABOUT CHOICES. BUT THERE IS MORE to this biblical lesson. Choices make us aware of the duality in which we live, in which we were created. But we also know that God is one. So we learn that our mission is to make this duality into a unity, a oneness. The task implied in Moses's instruction is to love God with both sides of your heart. We are somehow to love God with both our good inclination and our evil inclination. We are charged to remember that both were created by God and that both have a purpose.

The Jewish festival of Purim celebrates this idea. On Purim, one is commanded to get so drunk that one doesn't know the difference between "Blessed be Mordechai" (the hero of the Book of Esther) and "Cursed be Haman" (the villain). Why? Because evil has a purpose. Pain and death often cause us to think more deeply about who we are and what we are doing with our lives. Were it not for evil, how many of us would be stirred to action? Most of us would sit around in comfort, luxuriating in our apathy. Were it not for the visible presence of evil in the world, how many of us would work to combat it, whether in our world or in ourselves?

The challenge of loving God with our evil inclination is to find a way for it to serve good. If you are a hot-tempered person, why not use your anger to fight injustice? Your hot temper will find itself turning to passion for the cause you advocate.

I know of one such person, a young reporter, whose life was turned upside down when his marriage ended in divorce. He had wanted children; his wife had wanted a career. He was highly successful; try as she might, she had not been able to reach his level of fame as a writer. In the end, he had learned that she was being unfaithful to him. By the time the divorce decree was handed down, he was filled with bitterness not only toward his wife but toward all women. He wanted to get away from his world, and he found a way to do so—by accepting an assignment as a foreign correspondent in Asia.

Here was a man whose evil inclination could have pushed all his buttons. Yet he found a way of making that evil inclination serve

God and goodness in the world, though I doubt he would use those words to describe what happened.

His anger and bitterness, and his desire to flee from emotional pain, drove him to take risks and go places where no sane man would have gone. He brought out story after story that exposed injustice. He was nominated for a Pulitzer Prize and won many other awards in journalism. One of his best efforts involved smuggling himself into an Asian country whose leader was personally appropriating U.N. funds that were intended for malnourished children. The reporter documented that the children who were allegedly getting this special aid were, in fact, starving. This journalist's anger turned to passion, and with it he changed the world.

That is what it means to serve God with all your hearts. That is what it means to serve God with all you have. All you need to do is set your imagination to work to figure out how you, too, can accomplish this within your own reality. The first step is making a choice to do so. I can't put it better than Moses did himself: *"I have put before you life and death, blessing and curse. . . . Choose life!"*

31

Never Alone

BY THE TIME MOSES MAKES HIS FAREWELL ADDRESS TO THE Israelites, all of his people have experienced enormous suffering and grief. As those born in slavery have died off, their children have had to cope with the loss of their parents.

Moses himself knows how devastating death and grief can be, because the incident that cost Moses his own entry into the Promised Land followed the loss of a loved one, his sister, Miriam.

As the story goes, immediately after the death of Miriam, the people had started complaining again about their lack of water. This was a familiar complaint, one Moses had heard many times over the years and one he had always handled successfully. But this time he could not cope adequately, and the consequences were dire.

The people's complaint came at a time when Moses was preoccupied with his personal grief. Miriam had been like a mother to him, and she was greatly beloved by him. She was clearly one of the most important people in his life. It was Miriam who had watched the baby Moses in the waters of the Nile, following the little basket and risking her life to approach the pharaoh's daughter's retinue. Young as she was she had spoken to the princess, suggesting that a Hebrew woman care for the foundling.

Miriam and Moses had been reunited when he returned to lead the Israelites out of slavery. After the Israelites had successfully crossed the Sea of Reeds, Moses had sung a song of jubilation with the men, while Miriam had led the women in song. She had continued to serve as an important figure to Moses throughout their wanderings in the desert. On one occasion, when she had crossed words with him and God had afflicted her with leprosy, Moses had pleaded with God to forgive her and cure her, even though she had insulted him.

Miriam had also been beloved by the people. Her name, tradition has it, meant "one who turns bitter water sweet," and the Israelites believed that it was because of her that they had always had miraculous access to drinking water. It is, therefore, no wonder that upon her death, they panicked over the water situation, returning to their usual complaints.

This time Moses, commanded by God to speak to a rock from which water would flow, lashes out with his rod, striking the rock instead. His fury is apparent in the words he shouts at the people: *"You rebels, shall we get water for you out of this rock?"* These are not the words of Moses the kindly teacher, to whom the Israelites have grown accustomed. These are the words of an intolerant man overcome by grief.

It is interesting that when Moses calls his people "rebels," he chooses the Hebrew word *morim*, which, although pronounced differently, has the same spelling in Hebrew as "Miriam." This might be the first recorded instance of a Freudian slip. Like many people in modern society, Moses is caught up in a conflict between his multiple roles—that of a brother or family member and that of a leader of some three million people who depend on him to be strong no matter what happens.

I thought of this conflict when I read that Paramount Studios chairman Brandon Tartikoff had been forced to resign from his position following a terrible car accident in which his young daughter had suffered brain damage. Dealing with the guilt he felt for his role in the accident and trying to be involved in his daughter's rehabilitation had caused too much stress for this executive, whose duties demanded his undivided attention.

Tartikoff could resign and be replaced. Moses cannot. There is no one who can take his place. Moses cannot even take time off, since he is a unique leader, needed and *"trusted at all times in My home."* Moses's mistake in placing his personal emotions ahead of his responsibilities as a leader of his people costs him dearly.

God tells him that he is not fit to lead the people into the Promised Land, although He does mitigate this rebuke by taking Moses to the top of a mountain from which he can see the land his people will enter. At this juncture, a remarkable thing happens.

Since we were introduced to Moses back in the Book of Exodus, we have heard a particular phrase repeated over and over; indeed, it is repeated 175 times in the Bible, namely, "And God spoke to Moses, saying . . ."

Suddenly, we get the opposite: *"And Moses spoke to God, saying . . ."* Why?

When need be, Moses does not only listen, he knows how to speak up. This is a theme we have seen before in the Bible, and here we are again reminded that sometimes it is necessary for us to stand up and bring something to God's attention. Seeing the Promised Land and imagining his people crossing into it, Moses sees what will be needed, and he has the courage to speak up about it to God.

Moses tells God that a successor must be appointed to replace him, a successor whose right to leadership will be clearly established before the journey into the Promised Land begins. Perhaps Moses had learned in the court of the pharaoh how great kingdoms and great religions had been split and even lost because disagreements had erupted over the right of succession. Indeed, this is a frequent failing that we have seen innumerable times in the common era and that has afflicted many nations and ideologies. So Moses takes steps to forestall such a thing happening to his people.

Yet it must have been very hard for a man who was still so vital and strong to appoint a successor. Very few can do it. Many people are unable even to prepare their wills. It is difficult for them to imagine themselves gone and someone else, even a beloved someone else, ruling over their possessions.

I know of one father who brought his son into his company, intending to turn over the reins. But he found himself unable to relinquish power, and he ended up constantly hanging around, looking over his son's shoulder, questioning his son's decisions. Unable to take the stress, the son left the company, investing his money and energy elsewhere. When the father was eventually forced to retire due to ill health, the company he had spent his life building up "for his son" was sold to strangers. He lived to see how his inability to put aside his own ego had cost him everything he had held so dear: his company and his relationship with his son.

But Moses is able to put the future needs of his people above his own ego. When God tells Moses to appoint Joshua by laying his hand on him, Moses demonstrates that he is passing all his power to his successor with complete confidence by laying *both hands* on Joshua.

This is a significant lesson. How often do we anoint our leaders with both hands? Does it ever happen anymore? In the United States, over the course of the last thirty years, we have conferred power on our chosen leaders with only one hand. No sooner is a president elected than the criticisms start, not only from members of the opposing party but from the very people who voted for him. We don't seem to vote with confidence anymore, and accordingly, it is no wonder that our leaders don't seem to lead with confidence.

But confidence in leadership and a clear line of succession are not Moses's only concerns. Well aware of the pitfalls that come with exaggerated grief over the loss of someone near and dear, Moses is trying to ensure that his people will never feel totally alone.

The appointment of Joshua ensures that the Israelites will never be without a leader. Then Moses tells them something else—that they will also never be without a parent.

Remember that all these young people had recently lost their parents. These losses had left them not just grief-stricken, but also guilt-ridden, since, to some extent, they had to have been waiting for their parents to die. After all, they could not really get on with their lives, entering the Promised Land, until all the slaves had died.

Now Moses takes the grief and the guilt away. He tells them, *"You are the children of the Lord your God."* And he adds, *"You shall not gash yourselves nor make any baldness between your eyes for the dead. For you are a holy people to the Lord."*

Because you are the children of God, he is saying to them, the ancient practices of mourning are forbidden to you. You may not mutilate yourself or do yourself symbolic or psychological harm as a result of your loss. Your biological parents might have died, but you are not alone. God is your parent, and He will never abandon you.

Moses is well aware that he himself had forgotten that. When his surrogate mother, Miriam, died, he was overcome with grief and failed to live up to his responsibilities. Now, having realized his error, Moses ensures that his people learn this lesson well: You are never alone; you are the children of God.

For many people, this knowledge often creates a boundary between sanity and madness, between being able to accept the death of a loved one and being literally unable to go on.

I once officiated at the funeral of a woman whose husband was so grief-stricken that, as the casket was being placed in the grave, he threw himself onto it, screaming, "My wife—my life—has died!" It took a great effort on the part of family and friends to lead him away from the cemetery.

It is not uncommon to see people suddenly stricken with mysterious illnesses after the death of a spouse or other loved one. Indeed, a study by the National Institute of Mental Health shows that about 50 percent of primary mourners become ill or hospitalized during the first year following a loved one's death.

Obviously, people who cannot live without a loved one, who feel so utterly alone, have not really incorporated the concept that they will never be alone if God is with them. This is the point Moses is making so strongly in his farewell address: When you lose your mother and your father, you are not an orphan, because you are a child of God. God is your father and your mother.

As a psychologist, I try to build on this message of Moses's. When clients come to me speaking of their "inner child," I encourage them to try also to find their "inner parent."

If you have grown up with a mother or a father who was a poor role model, you need not be held back by your negative childhood experiences. The trick is to draw upon your own internal resources in an effort to create a nurturing parent within yourself. Clearly, this is not easy to do, but it becomes easier if you can perceive yourself as a child of God and live your life with that perception as a guiding principle.

Furthermore, by considering yourself a child of God, you will grow and develop into the person you really can be. As we discussed in Chapter 2, this psychological process, called "individuation," means that you can't be who you are meant to be until you individuate, or separate psychologically from your parents. Ultimately, this is the best way to honor your parents: to grow and develop into the best possible you.

I meet countless people who remain stunted in their growth as a result of their childhood experiences. It is as if they carry their parents around with them in their heads, constantly hearing the voices of negativity that made them shrivel up as children.

It is particularly tragic when grown adults take the image of their parents into their bedrooms, thus infecting their sexual relationships. A few clients have shared with me the observation that when they are in bed with their spouses, they wonder how many other people are actually present. A good marriage is predicated on leaving one's parents both physically and psychically. We learned in the very beginning of the first book, the Book of Genesis, that *"Hence a man shall leave his father and mother and cling to his wife, so that they become one flesh."* As we near the end of the last book, the Book of Deuteronomy, we are again reminded that we must leave our parents behind. As children of God, we must proceed with confidence into the unknown, into the Promised Land that is ours to claim. We are not traveling alone.

32

Secrets

As MOSES COMES TO THE CONCLUSION OF HIS ADDRESS, we notice that his language becomes more strident, the words clearly chosen to add emphasis to the message. His tone reaches a crescendo as he begins to list the transgressions that will bring a curse upon the people.

We have already seen in a number of instances what the Bible means by a curse. Remember when the Israelites, after cohabiting with Moabite women, began to worship the idols of Baal Peor? A plague was unleashed that killed 24,000 people. Clearly, a curse is a terrible calamity, and it is a strong word for Moses to use.

It is a fascinating choice when we look at the original text. In Hebrew, the word for "curse" is *ohrur*. And it is no accident that *ohrur* is related to the word *ohr,* meaning "light," which we first saw in the opening sentences of Genesis, discussed in Chapter 1.

Ohr is the powerful life force, the positive energy that is essential to our existence. But now, near the end of the Book of Deuteronomy, we are told that there is another force out there, a dark force, a negative energy that is toxic to life. That force is *ohrur*.

We have seen the Bible take words that mean something positive and alter them to emphasize something negative. In Chapter 27, we saw the relationship between the Hebrew words for "sanctity of marriage"—*kidushin*—and "harlot"—*kedeshah*. Thus, by changing a letter in a word, the Bible illustrates how sex can take you in the direction of sanctity or sin, the key difference being your mind-set and your partner.

In the case of *ohr* and *ohrur*, the difference also revolves around a person's mind-set, as we are about to see.

• *"Cursed be anyone who makes a sculptured or molten image . . . and sets it up in secret,"* Moses declares.

Here, the Bible is talking about a person who, on the outside, in public places, appears to be very religious and scrupulously observant. But secretly he worships idols, either by actually praying to them in private or by worshiping false values in his heart.

Of course, today the idols are not golden calves; they are one's bank account or one's ego or one's physical fitness. Any obsession that takes precedence over God can, and usually does, become an idol.

Idolatry, by whatever name, would be bad enough in itself, but here the Bible singles out the idolatry that is practiced *in secret.* This aspect is what brings on the curse. It is the mind-set of hypocrisy that is so abhorrent.

• *"Cursed be he who dishonors his father or his mother."*

Again, the concern is not about public disrespect but rather private, secret disrespect. How can you dishonor your parents secretly? In your heart.

Let's say you have to invite your mother for dinner. You don't want to do it, you even resent having to do it, but you do so anyway out of a sense of duty. You do it because you don't want to deal with your guilt if you don't invite her. Do you think your mother doesn't feel your resentment as you bring her into your house and then bury your nose in a newspaper so you don't have to talk to her? Do you think she isn't hurt?

Although the Bible doesn't specifically mention other relatives, I believe that it is equally possible to dishonor one's spouse or one's children in the same way. If a husband says "I love you" to his wife but in his thoughts doesn't mean it at all, the wife is bound to sense the dissonance.

In the movie *Hook,* Steven Spielberg's story of a grown-up Peter Pan, there is a good example of this phenomenon as it applies to children. A busy father promises his son that he will watch the boy's baseball game, but he gets caught up in a business deal instead. When the boy steps up to bat, his eyes search the bleachers for his father, but he sees only a man hired to videotape the event. It is clear that the father does intend to *watch* the game, as he had promised, but this technicality cannot assuage the son's hurt feelings at the moment when he needs his father's presence and emotional support.

- *"Cursed be he who removes his neighbor's landmark."*

Is the Bible so concerned about the physical boundaries of your neighbor's land? Yes, but I think it is even more concerned about the boundaries that surround your neighbor as a person. You must not infringe upon those personal rights, either externally or internally. People frequently behave properly while secretly infringing upon another person's rights. Consider the example of a person who, under the rules of affirmative action, hires a minority employee because he is legally obligated to do so. He follows the law to the letter, but in his heart he considers this person inferior to him. This is the kind of attitude the Bible curses here.

- *"Cursed be he who misdirects a blind person on the way."*

Would any of us maliciously give wrong directions to a blind person? Yes. We all do it from time to time. How often has a friend come to you for advice and you've told her what she wants to hear —knowing it's the wrong advice—simply because you don't want to be unkind? It's tough to tell a friend something unpleasant and risk a backlash. But if you know better, you are, in essence, misdirecting a "blind" person—perhaps not literally blind, but blind in her naïveté or lack of awareness of her behavior.

• *"Cursed be he who strikes his neighbor in secret."*

How is it possible to strike your neighbor in secret? With words. When you speak ill of another person, you are responsible for spreading negative energy. Harm is done even if the person never finds out. Harm is done even if what you said is true—particularly if, secretly in your heart, your motives were less than pure.

One example of the irreparable harm that can be caused by words is the case of one of my clients, a clergyman. Before seeing me, he had participated actively in a men's support group. At the outset of the group therapy sessions, it had been clearly indicated to all the members that the group would be a place for the open discussion of any issue and that all matters would be held in the strictest confidence. With that understanding, my client discussed some painful interpersonal conflicts he had experienced while counseling a bereaved couple whose child had died of leukemia. Even as he had officiated at the funeral and offered consolation to the grief-stricken parents, my client had sensed his own religious doubts and anger, but he had not known how to deal with these feelings.

Through another member of the group, these confessions were transmitted back to the grieving parents. It had been difficult enough for them to deal with their loss, but when the parents discovered that their clergyman had discussed his doubts with others, their anger with God was transformed into anger at their religious leader.

Not surprisingly, they shared their feelings of betrayal with some other members of their congregation, who in turn came forward to accuse the clergyman of a lack of faith, questioning whether he was fit to lead the congregation. His life was changed.

He found it difficult, if not impossible, to trust anyone again. Eventually, he decided to leave religious life and enter the business world.

Words can be as powerful as physical weapons. Negative energy transforms and infects all it touches. You can be sorry later and apologize all you want, but the damage is done. The poison has spread. That is why the Bible chooses to use this word, *ohrur,* which is the opposite of light. When we spread negative energy around, we bring darkness to others and to the world.

WHAT ABOUT GOOD PEOPLE WHO STRUGGLE TO OVERCOME THEIR evil inclinations, their shadow sides, and do good, even if they can't muster up the best of intentions in the process? Are they to be cursed as well? Perhaps knowing that such thoughts would cross the minds of his people, Moses is quick to point out, *"The secret things belong unto the Lord our God."* He means that the secrets of the heart will be judged by God.

We are created with vulnerabilities, weaknesses, and inclinations for good and bad. God judges us not according to what we start with but what we end with. God judges us on the basis of how deeply we struggle with the challenges that have been set before us. And only God knows and understands the depths of the struggles of each human being, the secret recesses of the heart, which no human being can judge.

So why such harsh admonitions from Moses? Because Moses has set himself a very high goal and, knowing that he is about to die, has neither time to waste nor words to mince. As a religious teacher, he longs to see the spiritual development of his people.

As any college student who has studied basic psychology knows, there are various theories of human development, such as Erik Erikson's stages of psychosocial development, Jean Piaget's stages of cognitive development, Lawrence Kohlberg's stages of moral development, and James Fowler's stages of faith development. The Five Books of Moses present the Bible's stages of spiritual development:

Stage 1 is the spiritual and emotional recognition that life is a struggle. In the Garden of Eden, humankind was presented with the choice between the tree of life and the tree of knowledge of good and evil, introducing the constant struggle between our good and evil inclinations.

Stage 2 is the decision to choose life by making a commitment to act ethically in accordance with God's commandments.

Stage 3 is the more complicated task of striving to become conscious of your unconscious side, of working on the secret part of yourself, so that your interior thoughts and intentions correspond to your exterior ethical behavior.

Stage 4 is the recognition that great tasks imply great risks which sometimes lead to great mistakes. However, a mistake is just a mistake—not damnation. During times when we stray from the path, we frequently experience feelings of alienation, loneliness, depression, and rage. Yet at those very moments we can also begin to discover that the Divine Presence is still with us. This realization becomes the prelude to the next stage of our spiritual journey: returning home.

Moses tells his people, *"When all these things befall you . . . and you return to the Lord your God, and you and your children heed His command with all your heart and soul, just as I enjoin upon you this day, then the Lord your God will restore your fortunes and take you back in love."*

These words describe and set the tone for the last stage of our spiritual development.

Stage 5 is an understanding of the meaning of atonement. In going astray, we embark upon a path that will ultimately lead to returning. We do not say, "Great is the person who has never fallen" but "Great is the person who has fallen and risen." You can always return. You can always come home. The door is always open. It is never too late.

In the last chapter, we discussed the fact that God never abandons His children. He is always with us, but when we choose to reject Him, we choose not to connect with His presence. When that happens, we feel it immediately, even if we deny it. We feel splintered, at odds with ourselves, at odds with everyone around us.

It is no accident that we call the process of returning to our connection with God "atonement." Look at that word. What does it spell? At-one-ment. When we return to God, we restore the broken connection; we make ourselves whole again. We are "at one"— with God and with ourselves.

Think about that for a moment. We are talking about being *at one with God*! To be at one with God means to be empowered to move mountains, to change the world, to take part in creation. Ultimately, that is what we are on earth to do. So why do so few of us ever realize this, much less succeed at this awesome task? The answer to that question comes next.

33

Transformation

THUS WE COME TO THE END OF THE FIVE BOOKS OF MOSES. Before we close our Bibles, however, let us take a moment to consider what we have learned, focusing particularly on what the stories of Moses, the Israelites' flight from Egypt, and their forty years of wandering in the desert have taught us.

Like many students of the Bible, I am taken with the story of Moses's transformation. First, he is transformed from a threatened child into a pampered prince. Next, he is transformed from a pampered prince into a man of action, who is so moved by the cruelty inflicted on a poor slave that he reacts in righteous anger. Then, he is transformed from a fugitive to a humble shepherd. Finally, he is transformed from a loner who dwells in the wilderness with his flocks to the leader of a nation.

If we look back on our own lives, we can all identify points of personal transformation—from childhood to adulthood, from college student to businesswoman, from bachelor to husband, from middle age to old age, from CEO to retiree. What makes Moses's transformations different from the usual transformations we experience is that every step that Moses took brought him closer to a union with God. His life decisions were not dictated by calculating the earning potential of his next career choice but by an overwhelming passion to bring justice into the world, to bring God into the world. Yet Moses was just as human as we are. That is why he is such a powerful example for us.

Remember when God spoke to Moses from the burning bush? It is a dramatic scene, hard to forget. It is clear that Moses understood that he was speaking to God Himself. If he had any doubts, they were erased by the subsequent miraculous transformation of his rod into a snake and back into a rod again. Yet after that demonstration—even knowing he was addressing God—Moses declined the mission God had offered him.

You see, Moses had a stuttering problem, and when he realized that confronting the pharaoh would require him to speak eloquently, his insecurity got the better of him. *"O Lord,"* he begged, *"I am not a man of words. . . . I am slow of speech, and slow of tongue."*

We know that eventually Moses did accept his mission and went on to fulfill it. Not only that, but his farewell speech turns out to be the longest farewell speech ever recorded. It begins, *"These are the words that Moses spoke . . ."* Clearly, he, who had not been a man of words, had become a man of many words.

This is an inspirational example, teaching us that we all start life with some sort of handicap—a slow tongue, a clubfoot, a harelip, painful shyness, or some other emotional vulnerability, which we either are born with or acquire in childhood. But, like Moses, we are all given the chance to overcome it.

How? One way is to focus our attention away from our vulnerability, away from ourselves, and to direct ourselves toward a cause that is greater than we are—a cause such as bringing justice or peace or compassion into the world, one that will consume us so passionately that we'll leap past the obstacles.

The worst handicap is the one we impose on ourselves by obsessing about ourselves. It is the handicap that has come to be known in America as the pursuit of individual happiness or the pursuit of success. Such an obsession is a trap that ensures that our handicaps will become magnified.

Viktor Frankl, in the introduction to *Man's Search for Meaning*, explains this concept:

> Don't aim at success—the more you aim at it and make it a target, the more you are going to miss it. For success, like happiness, cannot be pursued; it must ensue, and it only does so as the unintended side-effect of one's personal dedication to a cause greater than oneself or as the by-product of one's surrender to a person other than oneself. Happiness must happen, and the same holds for success: you have to let it happen by not caring about it. I want you to listen to what your conscience commands you to do and go on to carry it out to the best of your knowledge. Then you will live to see that in the long run—in the long run, I say!—success will follow you precisely because you had *forgotten* to think about it.

In the long run—when you are in the middle of an impassioned speech denouncing injustice or anti-Semitism or racism or cruelty to animals—your stutter will disappear, and you won't even notice. That is what happened to Moses.

I know a remarkable man who, like Viktor Frankl, is a survivor of the Holocaust. Incredibly, all the atrocities that he witnessed and endured did not destroy his humanity or sense of compassion for others. He has seen evil face to face and been tormented by the Nazis, yet he can still see goodness in all people. He is a loving family man and community leader. His spirit has won out over the handicap of his wartime experiences because he chose to be a victor instead of a victim.

I can cite another example, a woman client—let's call her

"Sharon"—who came to me to overcome a number of personal handicaps resulting from years of sexual abuse by her father. The most serious of these handicaps was her addiction to abusive situations. We tend to think of addiction as it relates to drugs or alcohol, but abuse can be as addictive as any other poison. The scarring Sharon had suffered as a child at the hands of her father had left her with such low self-esteem that she repeatedly entered relationships that only reinforced her own negative view of herself. She didn't realize that she was seeking abusive relationships because she didn't know how to live without them. But through therapy she began to see what she was doing and why, and her first transformation began.

Many more problems remained. When Sharon now went out on dates with men who treated her better, she would torture herself with questions about whether she should reveal her past and, if so, when. Her first attempts at achieving an intimate relationship were disastrous, and she realized that she could not hide her problems from herself or her partner. Eventually, however, she *did* learn how to deal with these issues, once she was no longer afraid of men or of her own sexuality. She ultimately found a spouse with whom she could share all aspects of life, including sensual intimacy.

When Sharon formed a family, it became the cause to which she could become dedicated, and she stopped obsessing about her own problems. Her mission was to raise children with high self-esteem, protected and free from the abuse that she had suffered.

The most remarkable part of her story is that in the end she was even able to forgive her father and treat him with respect. Her children, who were never left alone with their grandfather, nonetheless got to know him as a jovial person who showed them kindness and generosity. At great personal expense and self-sacrifice, Sharon was able to give her children a family connection that she felt would enrich their lives. Sharon refused to remain a victim and thus transformed herself into a victor.

Having gotten to know Sharon very well, I can assure you that she could not have achieved these feats of transformation had it not been for her relationship with God, which grew stronger as she grew stronger. The wonderful thing about God is that He is always there and we can always call on Him for help.

God heard Moses's complaint that he could not express himself well enough. God understood that Moses's transformation from a stutterer to an eloquent speaker could not happen overnight. So God gave him a helper: his brother, Aaron. Moses and Aaron went together to the Egyptian court, where Aaron helped Moses speak and perform miracles before the pharaoh.

Many of us are also given an Aaron in our lives, a family member, spouse, or friend, who brings out the best in us. The danger is that we may use this person as a crutch, but if we keep the relationship in balance, it can work as well as the partnership between Moses and Aaron.

It is interesting to note, however, that even in Moses's case, he does not blossom as a speaker until after his brother Aaron dies. When Moses does speak, tradition tells us that he speaks in seventy languages. Of course, this is not to be understood literally. The Israelites spoke Hebrew, and one language would have sufficed. What "seventy languages" means is that Moses speaks in seventy *ways;* that is, everything he tells the people in his farewell address has many layers of meaning.

In the introduction to this book, I quoted an ancient adage that there are seventy ways of reading the Bible, one for each year of one's life. As we learn and grow, this revered book will reveal shades of meaning and convey a new understanding for which we were not ready before.

I experienced this phenomenon myself while writing this book. My original manuscript was based on years of intensive study, personal analysis, life experience, and insights that had resulted from discussions with my students and clients. Yet as I readied the material for publication—editing, clarifying, and rewriting—I found new layers of understanding to convey. If I were to write this book next year, I would find still other ways of relating to the Bible based on additional experiences and insights. This is what the sages meant when they taught us that the Bible is a living book—it is as dynamic as the thirst for truth that we bring to it.

We can read the Bible as a story, concentrating on its surface meaning; we can read it more deeply, trying to find the message between the lines; we can read it as a series of sermons on how to live life; and we can read it for its hidden, mystical insights. This last way of reading the Bible requires us to reach deep within ourselves, connecting with the psychic reality within us. It requires us to see not only with our eyes but with vision.

In the final paragraphs of Deuteronomy, we are given a dramatic example of this kind of vision. Just before he dies, Moses ascends Mount Nebo, on the eastern bank of the river Jordan, just opposite Jericho, from which he can see the Promised Land. The Bible tells us, "*And the Lord showed him the entire land,*" going on to be very specific about how far Moses can see: "*Gilead as far as Dan, all Naphtali and the land of Ephraim and Manasseh, and the whole of Judah as far as the farthest sea, and the south and the plain—the Valley of Jericho, the city of palm trees—as far as Zoar.*"

Tourists who go to Jordan and climb Mount Nebo can readily attest that you can see next to nothing from this mountain. It is actually little more than a hill; you can barely make out Jericho. So how could Moses see all that?

The answer is that Moses was seeing with a special light, the supernatural light of *ohr*. He was seeing not just the physical Promised Land but the spiritual Promised Land. To put it another way, Moses was seeing the Promised Land that exists *beyond* the Promised Land.

The sages tell us that at that very moment Moses was privileged to see, by means of the divine light that had been created on the first day, a panoramic view of the entire history of humanity, from the beginning of time to the end of time. And then Moses saw the face of God.

Years earlier, shortly after the Exodus from Egypt, God had told Moses, *"You cannot see My face, for no person shall see Me and live."* This is why immediately after Moses sees God's face, he dies.

He dies *"by the mouth {kiss} of God."* Just as, at the beginning of Genesis, God created the first human being by breathing into him *"the breath of life,"* so here, at the end of Deuteronomy, God withdraws His breath from a human being with a kiss.

Moses's death is a beautiful example of total acceptance, the fifth and most difficult stage of death, which Elisabeth Kübler-Ross describes in her groundbreaking work on death and dying. Most dying people get stuck in one of the first four stages: denial, anger, bargaining, or depression. Very few people greet death with acceptance, realizing that this is the gateway to the Promised Land beyond the Promised Land. But we know that Moses had been granted that special vision, and he died with total acceptance.

A puzzling thing—an issue that has confounded biblical scholars—is that *Moses* tells us, *"And Moses died . . ."*

This has led some to conclude that Moses did not write the last few sentences of his farewell address, that Joshua wrote them. Yet the stories that have come down to us through tradition claim that he did—that he foresaw his own death and wrote about it with tears streaming down his cheeks.

For a long time, I was a proponent of the Joshua authorship theory. Then I had an insightful experience. I was called up for a biblical reading in my synagogue, escorting a friend of mine who was battling terminal cancer. I stood next to him as he chanted the blessing, and then this very passage about the death of Moses was read. I looked at him and saw that tears were rolling down his cheeks.

I understood then that my friend knew he would never again hear this passage read. He knew that the following year, when this same passage would be read again, he would not be here. Like Moses, he foresaw his own death, knowing that he would soon experience the kiss of God.

I put my hand on his arm, and, holding on to him, I understood how it had been possible for Moses to write that passage. I learned how it is sometimes impossible for us to understand the deep truths of the Bible until we *experience* them.

As I conclude this book, I wish you many inspirational experiences that will illuminate the Bible for you and that will allow you to see—not with your eyes but with vision—all of God's creation and your own role in it.

Conclusion

SO WE HAVE REACHED THE END, DEAR READER.

I hope the sampling I have offered here—which I do not present as either exhaustive or definitive—will unlock for you some of the secrets of this most ancient source. And I hope it will allow you to see how the Bible can be a most modern guide to life.

If you have read this far, it probably means that you already feel, on some level, the Bible's magnetic pull. To bring its magic fully into your life, all you have to do is say, "I am ready."

If you were to say this in Hebrew, you would need just one word: *hineni*. This is the word Moses used when God first spoke to him from the burning bush. The Bible recounts, *"He gazed, and there was a bush all aflame, yet the bush was not consumed. Moses said, 'I will turn to look at this marvelous sight; why doesn't the bush burn up?' When the Lord saw that he had turned to look, God called to him out of the midst of the bush, and said, 'Moses! Moses!' And he answered: 'Hineni.'"*

This is also the word Abraham used when God issued the supreme challenge to him—to sacrifice his beloved son, Isaac. The Bible recounts, *"And it came to pass, some time afterward, and God put Abraham to a test. And He said to him, 'Abraham,' and he answered, 'Hineni.' "*

You might have noticed that among all the biblical episodes we have examined in this book, we have not as yet discussed the story of the binding of Isaac. It is a troublesome story.

Why does God test Abraham *after* He has made His covenant with him? Surely, God knew He could trust Abraham *before* He entered into that covenant. Why would God demand something so incomprehensible from someone as kind and loyal as Abraham?

Many people have rejected religion because they could not reconcile the picture of little Isaac on the altar, his father wielding a knife above him, with the picture of God as a loving being.

If you are one of those who has been adversely affected by this story, consider that Isaac was no small boy at that time. Tradition suggests that he was thirty-seven years old and an active participant in this rite. In a world where people routinely sacrificed their children to appease the gods, the God of Abraham had an angel restrain Abraham's hand. This God—the one God—tells us very clearly that human sacrifice is precisely what He *does not* want. All He wants is to hear us say, "I am ready."

What exactly are we to be ready for? To accept our role in the cocreation of the world.

Remember back in Genesis, when God created the world and rested? The Bible tells us, *"And God blessed the seventh day and declared it holy, because on it God ceased from all the work of His creation that He had still to do."*

He had *to do?* What can that possibly mean?

It means that God hadn't finished creating. There was more left for Him to do, but He also wanted us to be His partners in the ongoing creative process.

We are all charged with the task of being God's partners in continuing the work of creation, in the fixing of the world. Every one of us is called on to participate in this work, but very few of us answer, *"Hineni."*

It doesn't matter who you are, what you have done or not done in the past. As long as you answer "I am ready" whenever the call comes, you can begin the process of transformation that will truly allow you to change the world.

I am reminded here of the story of Oskar Schindler, told so movingly in the movie *Schindler's List*. Schindler was a German industrialist facing financial difficulties. One would have to be generous to call him an entrepreneur; it would be more accurate to call him a con man. Yet this man, who had cared only for himself for so long, one day answered, *"Hineni."*

As a result, he saved thousands of people from the Nazi gas chambers. He didn't start out to do so immediately; he grew into this mission. Yet it absorbed him to such an extent that in the end, when those he saved thanked him for saving their lives, he broke down in tears, thinking only that, if he had just tried harder, he could have saved even more lives.

His people gave him a ring with an inscription from the Talmud that read, "He who saves even one life has saved the whole world."

So set yourself a small task. Do not aim to save the whole world. Save one life. Save yourself. It will be as if you saved the entire world.

When the call comes, you need only say, *"Hineni"*—I am ready.

Bibliography of English Translations
of the Hebrew Bible

The Five Books of Moses. New York: Schocken, 1995.

The Holy Scriptures. Philadelphia: Jewish Publication Society, 1917.

The Holy Scriptures. Jerusalem: Koren, 1989.

The Living Torah. New York: Maznaim, 1981.

The Pentateuch. New York: Judaica Press, 1990.

The Pentateuch and Haftorahs, 2d ed., J. H. Hertz, ed. London: Soncino, 1989.

Tanakh: The Holy Scriptures: A New Translation. Philadelphia: Jewish Publication Society, 1985.

Biblical References

ABOUT THE AUTHOR

RABBI LEVI MEIER, Ph.D., is the Jewish Chaplain at Cedars-Sinai Medical Center and a clinical psychologist in private practice. He and his wife, Marcie, and their children reside in Los Angeles, California.